SECRET CODES

Nancy Cook

Developed by Washington MESA

Funded by the Discuren Foundation

DALE SEYMOUR PUBLICATIONS

Parsippany, New Jersey

MESA wishes to express its appreciation to the following people for their advice and assistance, without which this module could not have been completed:

Nancy Cook, Project Director
Washington MESA
University of Washington
Seattle, Washington

Sherrill Sarbo
Mathematics Teacher
Seattle Public Schools
Seattle, Washington

Neal Koblitz
Mathematics
University of Washington
Seattle, Washington

Chris Johnson
Washington MESA
University of Washington
Seattle, Washington

Washington MESA middle school mathematics and science teachers in Seattle, Spokane, Tacoma, Toppenish, and Yakima, Washington

Project Editor: Joan Gideon
Production and Manufacturing Coordinator: Leanne Collins
Design Manager: Jeff Kelly
Illustrative Art: Rachel Gage
Text Design: Michelle Taverniti
Cover Design: Dennis Teutschel
Cover Photograph: Paul Ambrose, Typewriter, (FPG)
Photo page 62: UPI/Corbis-Bettman

Dale Seymour Publications®
An imprint of Pearson Learning
299 Jefferson Road, P.O. Box 480
Parsippany, New Jersey 07054-0480
www.pearsonlearning.com
1-800-321-3106

Dale Seymour Publications® is a registered trademark of Dale Seymour Publications, Inc.

Funded by the Discuren Foundation. This material in part is based on work supported by Grant No. MDR–8751287 from the National Science Foundation; Instructional Materials Development; 1800 G Street NW; Washington, DC 20550. The material was designed and developed by Washington MESA (Mathematics, Engineering, Science Achievement); 353 Loew Hall FH–18; University of Washington; Seattle, WA 98195. Any opinions, findings, conclusions, or recommendations expressed in this publication are those of Washington MESA and do not necessarily reflect the views of the National Science Foundation.

ISBN 0-201-49607-0
4 5 6 7 8 9 10–ML–04 03 02 01 00

SECRET CODES

CONTENTS

INTRODUCTION

Secret Codes is one of the middle-grades instructional modules created and field-tested by the Washington MESA (Mathematics, Engineering, Science Achievement) project. Washington MESA operates on the premise that effective classroom materials should facilitate connections between classroom and real-world mathematics and science. Staff members and teachers work with scientists, mathematicians, and engineers to outline each module. Pilot modules are tested in middle school classrooms, then revised using feedback from the teachers.

The modules weave important mathematics themes with relevant, exciting science topics. The activities are based on current reform philosophies recommended by the National Council of Teachers of Mathematics' *Curriculum and Evaluation Standards for School Mathematics* and the American Association for the Advancement of Science's *Project 2061*. Students will

◆ learn by doing. The mathematics of cryptology comes alive when students encode and decode messages to and from their classmates.

◆ employ a variety of reasoning processes by using several mathematics approaches to solve similar problems.

◆ learn to express technical concepts as they write and discuss answers to open-ended questions. The questions are designed to provoke further thought about how science and mathematics connect to the everyday world.

◆ learn the appropriate use of calculators by solving real problems. Students are taught how to conceptualize and set up problems that they can then solve using calculators.

◆ make connections between mathematics and science as well as connections within mathematics and science. Writing Link, History Link, Technology Link, and Interest Link activities are included to expand the connections to other subject areas.

◆ explore careers by simulating professional roles in the activities. Students also study jobs that use mathematics and science in the Career Link features.

Secret Codes directs middle school students toward active involvement in learning. Students emulate real-world work environments by collaborating in small groups and striving for group consensus. They work with concrete materials and evaluate open-ended problems—the combination that helps the transition from concrete to abstract thinking crucial to the intellectual development of students at this age. To ascertain that instruction is working, assessment is integrated into *Secret Code* activities. Assessment and instruction goals are identical.

Family encouragement can help students to succeed educationally, so a special activity involves students' families in hands-on, collaborative work. Students learn as they work with parents and family members in studying different cryptosystems.

Each activity begins with an Overview page summarizing what students will be doing and how the teacher needs to prepare. This is followed by background information for the teacher's use and a Presenting the Activity section, which describes the activity in detail and suggests discussion and assessment questions. This is followed by Student Sheets and Transparency Masters in blackline master form. (Completed Student Sheets are provided on pages 120–136.) Career Link, History Link, Writing Link, Technology Link, and Interest Link features are found throughout the book.

CONCEPTUAL OVERVIEW

Secret Codes addresses the following mathematics topics, science topics, and NCTM standards.

NCTM Curriculum Standards

Problem Solving
 Open-Ended
 Multiple Strategies
Communication
 Verbal and Written
Reasoning
 Logical and Spatial
 Predictions and Evaluations
Mathematical Connections
 Among Topics
 To Real-World Contexts

NCTM Teaching Standards

Worthwhile Tasks
 Real-World Contexts
Teacher's Role
 Listening and Observing
 Orchestrating Discourse
Enhancement Tools
 Calculators
 Concrete Materials
Learning Environment
 Collaborative Work

NCTM Evaluation Standards

Alignment
 Integral to Instruction
Multiple Sources
 Oral and Written
 Individual and Group
Multiple Methods
 Instructional Planning
 Grading
Mathematical Power
 Communicating
 Reasoning
 Integrating
 Generalizing

Mathematics Content

Number Relationships
 Primes
 Factors
 Equivalency
 One-to-One Correspondence
 Randomness
Number Systems
 Modular Arithmetic
 Commutative and
 Associative Properties
Computation and Estimation
 Modular Addition
 Modular Multiplication
 Calculators

Patterns and Functions
 Repeated Patterns
Algebra
 Linear Equations
Geometry
 Congruency
 Rectangles
 Construction
 Angle Measurement
Spatial Relationships
 Rectangles, Factors,
 and Primes
Statistics
 Frequencies
 Inferences

Science Topics

Cryptography
 Encoding
 Decoding
 Keys
 Keywords
 Security
 Coding Tools
Scientific Process
 Predicting
 Hypothesizing
 Analyzing
 Concluding

ACTIVITY OVERVIEW

Overview

Middle school students are intrigued with secret codes, spies, and mysteries. Many have developed secret codes of their own at one time, but they probably are not familiar with the actual codes used to exchange secret information currently and historically. In addition, they might not be aware of the mathematical structure of the codes. In *Secret Codes,* students explore the mathematics involved in cryptology by devising, enciphering, and deciphering codes.

The material in *Secret Codes* is presented in a problem-solving mode. Each type of code is introduced via an encoded message that students need to decipher, as though they are breaking "the enemies" secret messages. This module never gives codes to students. Throughout the module, discussion should focus on how easy it is to decipher a message if you know the code compared to how hard it is to break an unknown code. For example, if friends agreed on a code for exchanging messages just between themselves, they would want a code that they could encode and decode with ease, but that others who might accidentally see the message could not easily decode.

Secret Codes gives students a sampling of activities that *cryptographers* (people who write in code or study cipher systems) do, as well as an introduction to the mathematics involved in developing the cryptosystems (the method that changes words in and out of coded form). In studying secret codes, students learn about modular arithmetic and equivalency, and they use their knowledge of prime numbers and factors as they investigate different methods of encoding and decoding private information.

If possible, invite a cryptographer, a mathematician, or a computer scientist who specializes in security systems to visit the class to answer questions about secret codes.

Activity 1: Additive Ciphers

Students are introduced to additive ciphers of the sort in which A is replaced with D, B is replaced with E, and so on. Working in small groups, they explore the Caesar Cipher, one of the earliest known ciphers. They construct a replica of an early enciphering machine and use it in their investigations of other additive ciphers. Students discover the mathematical rules—the equations—for these well-known simple ciphers as they compose, encode, and decode messages to and from their classmates.

Activity 2: Modular Arithmetic

Students assign numerical values to the letters and develop encoding rules for numeric data. They investigate modular arithmetic in depth, including identity elements for addition and multiplication, additive and multiplicative inverses, commutative and associative properties, and the significance of prime bases, particularly in cryptology (the science of encoding, decoding, and deciphering messages).

Activity 3: Multiplicative Shifts

Students have become familiar with additive ciphers of the nature $C \equiv P + k \bmod 26$, where C is the coded equivalent of the plaintext P (original message) and k is any integer. They next turn their focus to multiplicative shifts in which $C \equiv P \times k \bmod 26$. The significance of primes again comes into view. They are critical to the development of codes that result in one-to-one correspondence between the original message (the plaintext) and the coded messages (the ciphertext). Students discover that there are limited numbers of multiplicative shifts that can be used in creating codes. The basis of determining which shifts are usable lies in relatively prime numbers.

Activity 4: Prime Numbers

Students search for all the prime numbers between 1 and 100. Using square tiles, they form all the unique rectangles they can that have an area of n square units, for $n = 1, 2, \ldots, 100$. They also determine the factors for each n, and then explore the relationship between number of unique rectangles, the dimensions of the unique rectangles, and factors. They determine which numbers are prime and which are composite, and they explore the *prime sieve*, a method to identify the primes between 1 and 100.

Activity 5: Affine Ciphers

Affine ciphers are a combination of additive and multiplicative ciphers resulting in the form $C \equiv a \times P + b \bmod d$. The encoding of affine ciphers presents no difficulty to middle schoolers, but the decoding, other than by trial-and-error if you do not know the encoding rule, requires solving two equations in two unknowns. Therefore, affine ciphers are quite secure to most middle schoolers—their friends and family will not be able to break this cryptosystem. For those who want to know how to break these ciphers, the information is given.

Activity 6: Vigenère Ciphers

The *Vigenère Cipher* is no more than a combination of multiple additive ciphers, but it forms the basis of a most secure cipher, the Vernam Cipher, which is still in use today. It will be explored as the Family Activity. The Vigenère Cipher consists of a keyword in addition to the multiple additive ciphers. An oversimplified description is that not all letters in the plaintext are encoded with the same additive cipher. This results in a polyalphabetic cipher, one in which there is no one-to-one correspondence between the letters in plaintext and ciphertext. It can, however, be cracked. Many middle schoolers will be excited about the Vigenère cipher.

Family Activity: Worms and One-Time Pads

Students review with their families the Caesar Cipher, letter frequencies, and additive ciphers. Very long keywords, equal in length to the plaintext, are introduced by having the family decode a ciphertext encoded using a line from a Link as the keyword. The *Vernam Cipher* is a Vigenère Cipher with one very important extension—the keyword in a Vernam Cipher is a *worm*, a sequence of randomly selected letters, removing all influence of letter frequency. The Vernam Cipher is commonly known as the *one-time pad*. It has a significant history, and it is still in use today.

MATERIALS LIST

The following is a consolidated list of materials needed in *Secret Codes*. A list of materials needed for each activity is included in the Overview for each activity.

Activity	Materials Required
Additive Ciphers	*For the teacher:* ◆ Transparencies of Student Sheets 1.1–1.5 *For each student:* ◆ Student Sheets 1.1–1.5 ◆ One piece of cardstock ◆ Construction compass ◆ Straightedge ◆ Brad ◆ Protractor
Modular Arithmetic	*For the teacher:* ◆ Transparencies of Student Sheets 2.1–2.5 *For each student:* ◆ Student Sheets 2.1–2.5 ◆ Calculator ◆ Sheet of grid paper *For each group of students:* ◆ Mathematics reference book
Multiplicative Shifts	*For the teacher:* ◆ Transparencies of Student Sheets 3.1–3.4 *For each student:* ◆ Student Sheets 3.1–3.4 ◆ The Alberti Enciphering Machine (from Activity 1) ◆ Calculator

Activity	Materials Required
Prime Numbers	*For the teacher:* ◆ Transparencies of Student Sheets 4.1–4.3 *For each student:* ◆ Student Sheets 4.1–4.3 ◆ Calculator *For each group of students:* ◆ 100 square tiles
Affine Ciphers	*For the teacher:* ◆ Transparencies of Student Sheets 5.1–5.2 *For each student:* ◆ Student Sheets 5.1–5.2 ◆ Calculator *For each group of students:* ◆ Mathematics reference book
Vigenère Ciphers	*For the teacher:* ◆ Transparencies of Student Sheets 6.1–6.2 *For each student:* ◆ Student Sheets 6.1–6.3 ◆ Calculator ◆ Alberti Enciphering Machine (from Activity 1)
Worms and One-Time Pads	*For each student:* ◆ Presenting the Activity Sheet ◆ Completed Student Sheet 1.2, 6.1, and 6.2 (for reference) *For each family group:* ◆ Family Activity Sheets 1–4 ◆ Interest Link "Steganography" (from page 112) ◆ Alberti Enciphering Machine (from Activity 1) ◆ History Link "One-Time Pads" (from page 111) ◆ Calculators ◆ Two dice, each of a different color

RESOURCES LIST

This list of resources was compiled by teachers, scientists, and professionals who participated in developing *Secret Codes*. It is intended for teachers who would like to pursue the topic further with their classes, for small groups of students who are particularly interested in the topic, for individual students who desire further investigations, or for the teacher's own professional development.

Beutelspacher, Albrecht. *Cryptology*. Washington, D.C.: The Mathematical Association, 1994.

Peck, Lyman C. *Secret Codes, Remainder Arithmetic, and Matrices*. Washington, D.C.: National Council of Teachers of Mathematics, 1961.

Kahn, David. *The Codebreakers*. New York: Macmillian, 1967.

Hilton, Peter. "Cryptanalysis in World War II—and Mathematics Education." *Mathematics Teacher* (October 1984).

Olivastro, Dominic. "Two Keys in a Code." *The Sciences* (July 1990).

Snow, Joanne R. "An Application of Number Theory to Cryptology." *Mathematics Teacher* (January 1989).

Reagan, James. "Get the Message? Cryptographs, Mathematics, and Computers." *Mathematics Teacher* (October 1986).

Luciano, Dennis, and Gordon Prichett. "Cryptology: From Caesar Ciphers to Public-Key Cryptosystems." *College Mathematics Journal* (January 1987).

Koblitz, Neal. *A Course in Number Theory and Cryptography*. New York: Springer-Verlag, 1994.

Rosen, Kenneth H. *Elementary Number Theory and Its Applications*. Reading, Mass.: Addison-Wesley, 1993.

ACTIVITY

1

ADDITIVE CIPHERS

Overview

Students are introduced to additive ciphers of the sort in which A is replaced with D, B is replaced with E, and so on. Working in small groups, they explore the Caesar Cipher, one of the earliest known ciphers. They construct a replica of an early enciphering machine and use it in their investigations of other additive ciphers. Students discover the mathematical rules—the equations—for these well-known simple ciphers as they encode and decode messages to and from their classmates.

Time. One to two 45-minute periods.

Purpose. Students discover the mathematical underpinnings of secret codes as they explore the relationship between encoding and decoding ciphertext.

Materials. *For the teacher:*

◆ Transparencies of Student Sheets 1.1–1.5

For each student:

◆ Student Sheets 1.1–1.5
◆ One piece of cardstock
◆ Construction compass
◆ Straightedge
◆ Brad
◆ Protractor

Getting Ready

1. Duplicate Student Sheets 1.1–1.5.
2. Locate cardstock, compasses, straightedges, protractors, and brads.
3. Prepare transparencies of Student Sheets 1.1–1.5.

Background Information

In this activity, students are introduced to *additive ciphers,* sometimes called *additive shifts*—coding systems in which each letter in the alphabet is substituted with another letter in a systematic way. For example, substituting each letter with the next letter in the alphabet (substituting B for A, C for B, D for C, and so on) is an additive cipher of shift 1. When you write the alphabet used in the message (called the *plaintext*) with the alphabet to be used in the coded message (the *ciphertext*) below it, you see that the alphabet for the ciphertext is shifted 1 to the left (or 25 to the right) of the alphabet for the plaintext.

Here is an additive cipher with shift 1:

Plaintext: A B C D E F G H I J K L M N O P Q R S T U V W X Y Z
Ciphertext: B C D E F G H I J K L M N O P Q R S T U V W X Y Z A

It is thought the Roman Emperor Julius Caesar was one of the first to use additive ciphers. The Caesar Cipher was an additive cipher of shift 3. He substituted D for A, E for B, F for C, and so on as shown below.

Plaintext: A B C D E F G H I J K L M N O P Q R S T U V W X Y Z
Ciphertext: D E F G H I J K L M N O P Q R S T U V W X Y Z A B C

Students might be familiar with this type of cipher, although they might not know it is called an *additive cipher* or a *Caesar Cipher.* Many secret messages in magazines, newspapers, and cereal boxes are forms of additive ciphers of varying shifts, including the Caesar Cipher.

There are 26 different additive ciphers—shift 1, shift 2, . . . , shift 26. Actually, a shift of 26 results in the original alphabet and is never used in creating secret codes! It is, however, a possible additive cipher.

There are two terms that need to be differentiated. The general rule for encoding the message, mathematically referred to as the *algorithm,* and the specific form of the rule that tells you exactly what to do, called the *key.* An additive cipher is a general type of coding procedure; it is an algorithm. The shift tells you exactly how far to shift each letter in the alphabet, and it is the key.

Student Sheet 1.1 introduces the Caesar Cipher. Students decode the following message:

ZKDW LV WKH PRVW IUHTXHQWOB XVHG OHWWHU LQ HQJOLVK?

Knowing that the Caesar Cipher involves an additive shift of 3, you can readily decode the message—"WHAT IS THE MOST FREQUENTLY USED LETTER IN ENGLISH?" Students, however, are not told the rule for the Caesar Cipher. They determine it.

This decoded message, focused on letter frequency, gets students thinking about the frequency of occurrence of the various letters in English. As you know, not all letters occur with the same frequency. Everyone is aware that *x, q,* and *z* are quite rare. While some students may know that *e* is the most frequently used letter in English, others might not. One of the most important tools in *cryptanalysis,* the deciphering of codes, is knowing which letters are most likely to be used. For example, in the ciphertext given on Student Sheet 1.1, H is the most frequently used letter. It occurs seven times. It is quite probable that H stands for E. It is the best first guess you could make, and in this case, it is the right guess. Once you know H stands for E, you might surmise that this is an additive shift 3 cipher, and based on this assumption, decode the entire message.

Most students will probably guess what the two- and three-letter words are and go from there. But once they know the frequency of letters in English, most students will incorporate that knowledge into their decoding strategies. Student Sheet 1.2 gives the approximate frequency of letter use in English.

On Student Sheet 1.3, students explore a different additive cipher— one of their own choosing.

On Student Sheet 1.4, students build a deciphering tool for additive ciphers. The Technology Link "The Alberti Enciphering Machine" gives more information about this tool.

Students use their enciphering machines on Student Sheet 1.5 to encode messages to exchange with their classmates, who must decode the ciphertexts. The use of the enciphering machines to both encode and decode messages will reinforce the inverse relationship between enciphering and deciphering.

The History Link "The Spartan Scytale" may be used at any time during this activity to further student interest.

Presenting the Activity

The Caesar Cipher. Some students will be more familiar and confident than other students with secret codes. To minimize these differences, group students in small groups based on compatibility. The group size is not important. Groups of two, three, or four all work well. Hand out Student Sheet 1.1, which is self-explanatory, and let groups work to decode the message.

As you circulate, notice how groups record the decoding and encoding rules. Many students will probably state "replace A with D," and so on. A few might write an expression, such as A → D, and maybe someone will mention modular arithmetic. The various rules will give you an indication of how familiar students are with the mathematics on which enciphering is based. At this point, simply observe their recordings. The mathematics will be formally introduced in Activity 2.

After decoding the message "What is the most frequently used letter in English?" students might want to find out the answer. If they do not come up with a strategy to determine which letter is most frequently used, suggest each student determine the most frequently used letter in a paragraph in a novel, newspaper, or magazine. The pooling of the results will probably lead to *e*. This is a good homework assignment.

Letter Frequencies.

When groups have finished decoding the exchanged messages and discussed within their groups the procedures they used, discuss the different strategies as a class. A discussion of the most frequently used letter in English will most likely arise, at which point you should either assign students the homework task of determining the most frequently used letters in English or hand out Student Sheet 1.2. It gives the letters by their approximate frequency of occurrence.

Me Caesar—You Decode.

Hand out Student Sheet 1.3. Make sure students understand that the Caesar Cipher is based on an additive shift 3 and that they are to encode a message based on an additive shift different from 3. The work is similar to that on Student Sheet 1.1, adding a discussion of the relationship between the encoding and decoding processes as well as a focus on the security of the code. You may need to elicit definitions of the words *secure* and *key* from students. After the groups have had time to discuss these two points, use a transparency of Student Sheet 1.3 for a class discussion of the different points of view.

Discuss the contrast between messages in which the key is not known (such as question 1 on Student Sheet 1.1) and messages in which the key is known (question 5 on Student Sheet 1.1). This discussion should be ongoing, and will be a major focus in some of the later activities.

The Alberti Enciphering Machine.

Student Sheet 1.4 gives instructions on how to build a replica of the Alberti Enciphering Machine. The procedure is quite clear. The only precision required is the division of each wheel into equivalent-sized arcs. If the size of the arcs vary greatly, it will be difficult to correctly align the wheels and readily translate from the plaintext to the ciphertext alphabet.

Circulate among the groups to ensure that students are correctly dividing the wheels. There are 360° in a circle, and this is to be divided into 26 equal-sized arcs, each being not quite 14°. Use a transparency of Student Sheet 1.4 to show how the diagram's arcs are spaced. Suggest students pencil in the arcs and rotate the wheels one space at a time, checking the accuracy of each arc before inking in the final lines.

This would be a good time to have students read the Technology Link "The Alberti Enciphering Machine."

Machines at Work. Hand out Student Sheet 1.5. Students will appreciate the potential of the enciphering machine as they put it to work. When the groups are ready, discuss as a class the relationship between the encoding and decoding processes.

Discussion Questions

1. Letters occur with different frequencies in English. What role does this play in cryptanalysis?

2. Does the frequency of occurrence of letters in other languages play a role in cryptanalysis?

3. What is the relationship between the encoding and decoding procedures?

4. Are additive ciphers secure codes? Would a ciphertext be easy to decode if you did not know the key?

Assessment Questions

1. Boris Badenuf communicates with Natasha using a plaintext alphabet of 26 letters plus a comma, a period, and a space.

   a. Design an enciphering machine for them.

   b. Write the rule you think Boris uses to send messages to Natasha.

   c. Dudley Doright intercepted one of their messages.
      Write the ciphertext.

2. Exchange ciphertexts from the first question with a classmate and decode it. Write the plaintext (the original message).

3. List the strategies used in decoding a message. Explain the importance of each.

Cryptic Terminology

This list defines most of the words used to talk about cryptology.

- Cipher: *n.* based on a system of changing the order of letters or words, or substituting letters or words with letters, words, numbers, or symbols according to a plan. *v.* to convert to ciphertext.

- Ciphertext: *n.* the coded form of plaintext.

- Code: *n. uses* signs, sounds, numbers, letters, or words to stand for letters, words, sentences, or complete thoughts. *v.* to translate a message to code, to encode.

- Cryptanalysis: *n.* solving the secret communications of other people without their permission. Solving a code or cipher.

- Cryptanalyst: *n.* someone who determines the code or cipher in order to translate a coded message.

- Cryptogram: *n.* a message in code or cipher.

- Cryptographer: *n.* someone who writes in code or studies codes and cipher systems.

- Cryptography: *n.* study and practice of the methods of communications security. The art and science of making communications unintelligible to all except the intended recipient. The means of encoding or enciphering communications.

- Cryptology: *n.* the technology of secret communication or the science that includes message concealment and then solving the message.

- Cryptosystem: *n.* the method that changes ciphertext into plaintext or the other way around.

- Decipher or decode: *v.* to convert a coded message into intelligible language.

- Decryption: *n.* the conversion of ciphertext into plaintext by the legitimate receiver.

- Encipher or encode: *v.* to convert a message into code.

- Encryption: *n.* the conversion of plaintext in ciphertext.

- Plaintext: *n.* the original message.

The Alberti Enciphering Machine

Leon Battista Alberti (1404–1472) had many talents. He was an architect, artist, musician, and writer. But he is famous not for his design of the Trevi Fountain or for his poetry, but for a little device made simply of two round pieces of copper. His invention is called the Alberti Enciphering Machine. It was the result of many years of work Alberti dedicated to *cryptography,* the study and practice of making messages secret.

Alberti created his enciphering machine in 1470. It was made out of two copper disks, one smaller than the other. They were fastened together at the center so the disks could rotate. The alphabet was written in the same order on each disk. Each of the 26 additive shift ciphers could be created by rotating one or the other disk. This was the first tool that could create many different ciphers. The picture below shows the Caesar Cipher.

Alberti's enciphering machine was not really appreciated by people in his time. Not until the nineteenth century did nations begin regular use of enciphered codes for military and political communication.

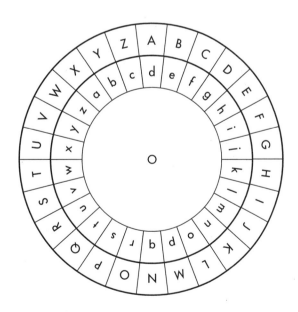

The Spartan Scytale

Before Caesar used his cipher to send secret messages, the Spartans in ancient Greece were using the first known cryptographic device. It was called the *scytale*.

The scytale was made of a cylinder and a strip of papyrus paper. The paper strip was wrapped in a tight spiral around the cylinder of wood, or sometimes around an officer's baton. Greek rulers would write messages down the length of the cylinder. When they unwound the paper, the letters of the message became jumbled. Couriers would then take these messages to commanders at Spartan battle camps. Even if enemies intercepted the message, they would not know how to put it back together because they did not have the right diameter of cylinder to realign the letters in their proper orders.

You can make a version of a scytale using long strips of half-inch wide paper and an empty paper towel roll. Wrap the paper strip around the cardboard roll so you cannot see the roll under the paper, but do not overlap it. Write your message across the roll, continuing the message under the first line by turning the roll. Unwrap the paper and send it to a friend. Make sure your friend has the same-sized cardboard roll to decipher the message!

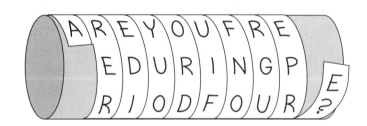

The Caesar Cipher

1. Caesar invented one of the earliest known secret codes. A secret code is also called a cipher. The following message was *encoded* (written in code) using the Caesar Cipher. Decode it and write it below.

   Z K D W   L V   W K H   P R V W   I U H T X H Q W O B   X V H G

   O H W W H U   L Q   H Q J O L V K ?

2. Describe the decoding rule for the above message.

3. Describe the encoding rule called the *Caesar Cipher*.

4. As a group, compose a message and write it below. Using the Caesar Cipher, encode your message and write it below. Also write the encoded message on another piece of paper.

5. Exchange coded messages with another group. Write the coded message you received below. Decode it and write the decoded message below the encoded one.

6. Discuss with your group the procedures you used to encode and decode the messages. Outline the critical points of the procedures you used.

Letter Frequencies

1. Not all letters are used with the same frequency in any natural language. In English, E is the most frequently used letter in novels and newspapers, occurring with a frequency of nearly 13 percent. The following table gives the letters by their relative frequencies of use in English.

Frequency of Use in English

Letters	Approximate Frequency of Each Letter
E	13%
T	9%
A, O	8%
I, N	7%
S, H, R	6%
D, L	4%
C, U	3%
M, W, F, G, Y, P	2%
B, V, K, J	1%
X, Q, Z	<1%

2. Cryptanalysis is the process of figuring out secret codes and ciphers. Discuss how knowing the frequency of use of the letters aids in cryptanalysis.

Me Caesar—You Decode

1. The Caesar Cipher is a shift. Each letter of the alphabet is replaced with the third letter after it. A → D, B → E, and so on. One way to write the rule could be:

   $P + 3 \rightarrow C$ where P is any letter in the plain alphabet and C is its coded form.

   Note that X + 3 → A, Y + 3 → B, and Z + 3 → C. The Caesar Cipher is an additive shift of $^+3$. It could also be described as an additive shift of $^-23$.

2. As a group, decide what shift you would have used, had you been Caesar. Write the rule for encoding a message with your shift.

3. As a group, develop a short (10-word, 75-letter maximum) message. Write the message below.

4. Encode the message with your modified Caesar shift. Write the encoded message below. Also write it on another piece of paper.

Me Caesar—You Decode

5. Exchange encoded messages with another group. Decode the message you received. Write both the encoded and decoded forms of the message below.

6. What is the rule for decoding the other group's message?

7. What is the rule that was used to encode the message?

8. What is the relationship between the encoding and decoding rules?

9. To say a code is *secure* means the coded message is very difficult to figure out for anyone who does not have the key. How secure is the other group's code?

The Alberti Enciphering Machine

1. Another word for *encoding* is *enciphering,* and *deciphering* is another word for *decoding*. If *enciphering* and *deciphering* are new words to you, check them out in the dictionary or in the Interest Link on page 6.

2. In 1470, Leon Battista Alberti invented a mechanical enciphering machine. It consists of two wheels, one bigger than the other, fastened together in the center so each wheel can freely rotate. The letters of the alphabet are written in the same order on each wheel. In one position, each letter on the outer wheel can be matched with the same letter on the inner wheel. You can rotate the wheel to create an additive shift of any magnitude. This picture shows the Caesar Cipher. The inner wheel is shifted three spaces to the left.

   You are going to build a replica of the enciphering machine.

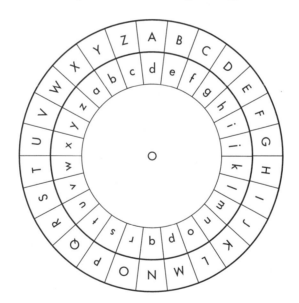

3. Get the following materials from your teacher.
   • One piece of cardstock
   • Construction compass and straightedge
   • One brass brad

The Alberti Enciphering Machine

4. Follow these directions.
   a. Decide on the size of the two wheels. Draw them on the cardstock with the compass and cut them out.
   b. Carefully determine the spacing on one of the circles, making sure you have 26 equally spaced arcs for the 26 letters. Once you are certain the spacing is correct, outline the spaces by drawing a line between them lightly with a pencil.
   c. Using the compass holes as a pattern, line up the circles, enlarge the compass holes, and fasten the circles together with the brass brad.
   d. Using a pencil, lightly outline the spacing on the second circle by carefully matching it to that on the first circle.
   e. Write the alphabet on each wheel. To reduce coding errors, it sometimes helps to put capital letters on one wheel and lowercase letters on the other wheel.
   f. Check to see that the spacing is correct for every letter. When you are sure, ink in the lines.

Machines at Work

1. As a group, compose a 20- to 30-word message. The message before it is encoded is called the *plaintext*. Write the plaintext below.

2. Decide on the code, which is also called a *cipher,* you will use. Write it below.

3. Using your enciphering machine, encode your message. The encoded message is called the *ciphertext*. Write the ciphertext below. Also write it on a separate piece of paper.

4. Exchange ciphertexts with another group. Using your enciphering machine, decode the ciphertext you received. Write both the ciphertext and plaintext below.

5. What is the decoding rule you used to decode this new ciphertext?

6. What rule did the other group use to encode the message?

7. What is the relationship between the encoding and decoding rules?

ACTIVITY
2

MODULAR
ARITHMETIC

Overview

Students assign numerical values to the letters and develop rules for encoding numeric data. They investigate modular arithmetic in depth, including identity elements for addition and multiplication, additive and multiplicative inverses, commutative and associative properties, and the significance of prime bases, particularly in cryptology.

Time. Two to three 45-minute periods.

Purpose. Students begin to learn of the extensive use of mathematics in cryptography. They learn that cryptosystems are basically mathematical systems, and they learn of a real-world use of modular arithmetic.

Materials. *For the teacher:*

◆ Transparencies of Student Sheets 2.1–2.5

For each student:

◆ Student Sheets 2.1–2.5

◆ Calculator

◆ Sheet of grid paper

For each group of students:

◆ Mathematics reference book

Getting Ready

1. Duplicate Student Sheets 2.1–2.5.

2. Locate calculators and mathematics reference books.

3. Prepare transparencies of Student Sheets 2.1–2.5.

Background Information

This activity begins with students assigning numerical values to the letters and developing rules for encoding numeric data. Students might naturally want to assign the values A = 1, B = 2, . . . , Z = 26, and this is a common system in cryptography. This system is introduced on Student Sheet 2.1.

Students also record the corresponding numerical values on their enciphering machines and determine the numerical rule that describes the Caesar Cipher. For example, consider the numerical value of Y = 25. The Caesar Cipher sends Y → B. The numerical value for B = 2. Students develop a numerical rule that sends 25 → 2, a process that leads into modular arithmetic.

Students know from Student Sheet 1.3 that the Caesar Cipher is an additive shift 3. Any letter P in the plaintext goes to P + 3 in the ciphertext. Symbolically, this could be written as $P + 3 → C$. For example, Y + 3 → B, or numerically, 25 + 3 → 2. Some groups might realize this is an example of mod 26 arithmetic; others might not, therefore, modular arithmetic is formally introduced on Student Sheet 2.2. The Interest Link "Modular Arithmetic" presents an overview of the process.

In mathematical terms, C the Caesar Cipher equivalent of P is defined as $C ≡ P + 3$ mod 26. The symbol ≡ stands for congruence. B does not equal Y, but B is the Caesar Cipher equivalent of Y. Similarly, in modular arithmetic, 2 ≠ 28, but 2 ≡ 28 mod 26.

Modular arithmetic is introduced with mod 26, which parallels the work students have been doing with alphabets. For an analysis of modular arithmetic, the focus shifts to a mod 7 system for two reasons: it is convenient and it is prime. A 7-by-7 matrix fits on a page in a readable size font, whereas a 26-by-26 matrix does not. A more important reason is that 7 is prime, and mod n systems for which n is prime have unique features.

Students make an addition table mod 7, given on the next page.

The *additive identity* is defined as the number i when added to any number n always results in n; in other words, the additive identity is i such that $n + i = n$. In ordinary arithmetic, the additive identity is zero; $n + 0 = n$. In mod 7 addition, the identity element with respect to addition is 7: $n + 7 ≡ n$ mod 7 for all n.

The *additive inverse* of n is that number p such that $p + n$ equals the additive identity. In ordinary addition, the additive identity is 0, so the additive inverse for p is ^-p. The additive identity mod 7 is 7, so the additive inverse for p is that number n such that $n + p ≡ 7$ mod 7. It can be readily determined from the mod 7 addition table. For example, 3 + 4 ≡ 7 mod 7, therefore, 4 is the additive inverse of 3 mod 7.

Addition Mod 7

+	1	2	3	4	5	6	7
1	2	3	4	5	6	7	1
2	3	4	5	6	7	1	2
3	4	5	6	7	1	2	3
4	5	6	7	1	2	3	4
5	6	7	1	2	3	4	5
6	7	1	2	3	4	5	6
7	1	2	3	4	5	6	7

A mod 7 addition table can be used to do mod 7 subtraction. For example, $4 + 5 \equiv 2$ mod 7. Subtraction is the inverse operation of addition, therefore, $2 - 5 \equiv 4$ mod 7 and $2 - 4 \equiv 5$ mod 7. These results can be read directly from the addition table mod 7. To determine what $3 - 4$ mod 7 is, locate the 3 in the body of the table that is in column 4, and determine what row it is in. The 3 in column 4 is in row 6. Therefore, $3 - 4 \equiv 6$ mod 7. You can verify the subtraction by performing the inverse operation addition: $4 + 6 \equiv 3$ mod 7. Note that $3 - 6 \equiv 4$ mod 7.

Student Sheet 2.3 provides space for students to construct a multiplication table mod 7. The *multiplicative identity* is that number i such that $n \times i = n$. The multiplicative identity is 1 in ordinary arithmetic, and it also is 1 in mod 7.

The *multiplicative inverse* of n is that number q such that $n \times q$ equals the multiplicative inverse. In both ordinary and mod arithmetic, the multiplicative inverse is 1, and it can be readily determined from the mod 7 multiplication table. For example, $3 \times 5 \equiv 1$ mod 7. Therefore, 5 is the multiplicative inverse of 3 mod 7.

A mod 7 multiplication table can be used to do mod 7 division. For example, $4 \times 5 \equiv 6$ mod 7. Division is the inverse operation of multiplication, therefore, $6 \div 5 \equiv 4$ mod 7 and $6 \div 4 \equiv 5$ mod 7. These results can be read directly from the multiplication table mod 7. To determine what $6 \div 5$ mod 7 is, locate the 6 in the body of the table that is in column 5, and determine what row it is in. The 6 in column 5 is in row 4, therefore, $6 \div 5 \equiv 4$ mod 7. Note that $6 \div 4 \equiv 5$ mod 7.

Multiplication Mod 7

×	1	2	3	4	5	6	7
1	2	3	4	5	6	7	1
1	1	2	3	4	5	6	7
2	2	4	6	1	3	5	7
3	3	6	2	5	1	4	7
4	4	1	5	2	6	3	7
5	5	3	1	6	4	2	7
6	6	5	4	3	2	1	7
7	7	7	7	7	7	7	7

On Student Sheet 2.4, students explore the properties of arithmetic operations. The commutative property of addition states that $a + b = b + a$, and it holds for modular arithmetic. For example, $4 + 5 = 5 + 4 \equiv 2$ mod 7. The associative property of addition, which states $(a + b) + c = a + (b + c)$, also holds for modular arithmetic. For example, $(2 + 4) + 5 = 2 + (4 + 5) \equiv 4$ mod 7.

The commutative property of multiplication also holds for modular arithmetic. For example, $5 \times 7 = 7 \times 5 \equiv 7$ mod 7. The associative property of multiplication also holds for modular arithmetic: $(4 \times 2) \times 3 = 4 \times (2 \times 3) \equiv 3$ mod 7.

On Student Sheet 2.5, students explore modular arithmetic in a non-prime modular system. Addition in a nonprime modular system is quite routine, there are no surprises. Multiplication in a nonprime modular system, however, is full of surprises. The rows and columns that involve a factor of the nonprime mod consist of many repeats.

For example, in the mod 6 multiplication table given on the next page, the rows and columns for 2, 3, and 4 have many repeats and no 1s. The only rows that have a unique value for each possible product are 1 and 5. One is a special number, and 5 is the only number between 2 and 5 that does not share a common factor with 6. In mathematical terms, 5 is relatively prime to 6.

In addition, a multiplicative inverse does not exist for each number. For example, there is no number n such that $n \times 2 \equiv 1$ mod 6. Another interesting fact is that division mod 6 is not unique: $3 \div 3 \equiv 1$ mod 6, $3 \div 3 \equiv 3$ mod 6, and $3 \div 3 \equiv 5$ mod 6.

Multiplication Mod 6

×	1	2	3	4	5	6
1	1	2	3	4	5	6
2	2	4	6	2	4	6
3	3	6	3	6	3	6
4	4	2	6	4	2	6
5	5	4	3	2	1	6
6	6	6	6	6	6	6

The Writing Link "Some Other Ciphers" may be used at any time during this activity to further student interest.

Presenting the Activity

Numerical Enciphering. Divide students in small groups. Groups of two, three, or four all work well. Hand out Student Sheet 2.1 and grid paper, and let groups incorporate numeric codes into their enciphering machines.

As you circulate, take notice of how the groups record the numerical rule for the Caesar Cipher. Students might write something similar to $P + 3 = C$. Some students might specify that P is the numerical value of a letter in the plaintext alphabet, and C is its equivalent value in the ciphertext alphabet. Some might use only numbers: $24 + 3 \rightarrow 1$. Others might add notes to describe what happens to X, Y, and Z, such as "$P + 3 = C$ for $n = 1, \ldots, 23$ and $P + 3 - 26 = C$ for $n = 24, 25, 26$." A few might write an equation involving notation for modular arithmetic, such as $P + 3 = C \mod 26$. The various notations used to write the rules will give you an indication of how familiar students are with modular arithmetic. At this point, it will suffice to observe their recordings. Modular arithmetic will be formally introduced on Student Sheet 2.2.

After students have had time to discuss within their groups real-world examples of shift 12, such as the standard notation for tracking time, orchestrate a class discussion to share examples and different suggestions for mathematical notations. At this point, elicit the details needed to clearly, but not necessarily efficiently or elegantly, symbolize the Caesar Cipher or any additive shift algorithm. This will lead to Student Sheet 2.2.

Mod Arithmetic. Have students read the Interest Link "Modular Arithmetic," then hand out Student Sheet 2.2. Ask groups to discuss question 1 to ensure that every member in the group understands modular arithmetic. While this will probably be a review for the majority of students, there might be a few for whom the material is new. Circulate to see that all students understand modular arithmetic. Use a transparency of Student Sheet 2.2 to work through a few examples if necessary.

As students are completing the addition mod 7 table, circulate among groups to ensure that all members understand the process. After students have completed the analysis of the table (question 7), discuss the addition mod 7 table as a class, eliciting from groups the fact that rows and columns 8, 9, and 10 are repeats of rows and columns 1, 2, and 3. They add no new information and could be omitted.

Have groups define the additive identity and continue the work on Student Sheet 2.2. If students do not immediately recall the meaning of additive inverse (requested in question 14), have them research it before completing the student sheet. When the student sheet is completed, discuss as a class the relationship between addition and subtraction, allowing students the opportunity to share their strategies for using a mod 7 addition table to do subtraction.

Multiplication Mod 7. Hand out Student Sheet 2.3. Circulate or use a transparency of this student sheet to make sure students understand multiplication mod 7. The work on multiplication mod 7 is analogous to that on addition mod 7. Help students understand the multiplicative identity and the multiplicative inverse. After the groups have completed the work on using the multiplication mod 7 table to do division mod 7, orchestrate a class discussion to bring out the different strategies.

Mod Arithmetic Revisited. Hand out Student Sheet 2.4. Students explore the commutative and associative properties of modular arithmetic. The work is self-explanatory. After students have completed it, ask groups to share with the class their examples and possible generalizations to other well-known properties, such as the distributive property.

Mod 4, 6, 8—What Do Spies Appreciate? On Student Sheet 2.5, students explore a modular nonprime arithmetic system. Hand out the sheet and without discussion, allow students to investigate the situation. Students will likely be quite surprised by the results of multiplication mod non-prime. Allow student groups to investigate the structure of the mod nonprime system. After they have discovered that division is not unique in this system, have a class discussion where students share their findings.

Elicit students' thoughts regarding the use of mod prime versus mod nonprime systems in cryptography. Students might point out that the Caesar Cipher was a mod nonprime system (26), and it seems to work. Elicit from the group that the Caesar Cipher is an additive cipher, and the nonuniqueness resulting from mod nonprime systems shows up in multiplicative ciphers, which we will study in the next activity.

Students might point out that a mod 7 system, even though it is prime, would not be good for coding messages in English. It would not yield a monoalphabetic cipher. Elicit students' ideas on why mod 7 was explored. Ask what length alphabet would lend itself to a mod 7 system. If they had a six-symbol alphabet, would they prefer a mod 6 or a mod 7 system?

What would be a good prime mod to use with English and what advantage would it have over mod 26? Students will not understand the full extent of this work on prime versus nonprime mod systems until they work with multiplicative ciphers in Activity 3, and this discussion is a perfect prelude to it.

Discussion Questions

1. Modular arithmetic is frequently called clock arithmetic or remainder arithmetic. Explain why each of these names would be used.

2. What is the minimum number of rows and columns needed to create a mod m addition table? A mod m multiplication table?

3. Prime numbers play a significant role in sophisticated cryptic systems. Why do you think this is so?

Assessment Questions

1. On Student Sheet 1.3, you used an additive cipher different from the Caesar Cipher. Write a numerical code for that cipher and give a few specific examples illustrating its use.

2. Create a new name for modular arithmetic and explain why it would be a logical name for the process.

3. Let a stand for your age. Create a mod a addition table and determine the additive identity. Give the additive inverse of $a + 1$. Create a mod a multiplication table and determine the identity element with respect to

multiplication. Give the multiplicative inverse of $a + 1$. Is division mod a unique? Give examples to support your argument.

4. Boris Badenuf is still communicating with Natasha using a plaintext alphabet of 26 letters plus a comma, a period, and a space.

   a. Incorporate a numeric code into the enciphering machine you designed for them.

   b. Write the numeric rule you think Boris uses to send messages to Natasha.

   c. Dudley Doright intercepted another of their messages, and it consisted of just numbers. Write the ciphertext and the plaintext.

Modular Arithmetic

In cryptography, it is common to assign numerical values to letters. For example, A = 1, B = 2, and so on. You can use these numerical values in coded messages through a form of arithmetic called modular arithmetic. Here is how it works.

You learned you can write a formula for the Caesar Cipher: $C \equiv P + 3$ where C stands for the ciphertext letter, P stands for the plaintext letter, and 3 is the amount of the "shift." The $\equiv$ symbol means "is congruent to." For example, B does not equal Y, but in the Caesar Cipher, B $\equiv$ Y. Let's say your plaintext has the letter A in it, and A is represented by the number 1. Then A = 1 = P. When you add 3, you get 4. Change the plaintext letter to the ciphertext letter that is assigned to 4 (the letter D). In this case, 1 $\rightarrow$ 4 or A $\rightarrow$ D. What about the plaintext letter Y? Using the formula, we get $C \equiv$ Y + 3 or $C = 25 + 3$. So $C = 28$. But there is no letter assigned to 28. So what ciphertext letter would you use?

This is where modular arithmetic comes in. We choose a mod number—a base number that will reflect how every letter is coded. Because there are 26 letters in the alphabet, let's choose mod 26. Here are the steps to change any letter in plaintext into a ciphertext letter in mod 26.

Modular Addition

1. Use the numerical value for letter in the plaintext. For example, Y = 25.
2. Follow formula.

3. Subtract 26 (modular value) until the difference is between 1 and 26.
4. C is the difference.

Caesar Cipher: $C \equiv P + 3$ mod 26

$P = 25$

$C = 25 + 3 = 28$ (but there is no letter assigned value 28)

$28 - 26 = 2$

$C = 2$ and this is $\equiv$ to the letter B.

Let's say you wanted to send a secret message to Rex. In plaintext, R E X is 18 58 24. In the Caesar Cipher, the R would become 18 + 3 = 21, which is U. E would become H.

Here's how you would numerically find the letter X using the above steps.

1. X = 24
2. C = 24 + 3 = 27
3. 27 − 26 = 1
4. C = 1 which is ≡ A

So REX in your plaintext message would become UHA in your ciphertext.

Modular arithmetic generally follows the same rules as regular arithmetic. For example:

If	$C \equiv P + 3 \mod 26$
so that	$1 \equiv 24 + 3 \mod 26$
then	$1 - 24 \equiv 3 \mod 26$
and	$1 - 3 \equiv 24 \mod 26$

You will investigate these rules for addition and multiplication in modular arithmetic as you work through Activity 2.

Some More Ciphers

In this module, you will learn about some mathematical ciphers that professional cryptographers use. Cryptographers are people who study or write codes or cipher systems. There are many ways to send secret messages. Have you ever tried to speak in pig Latin (igpay, atinlay)? That is a form of code. Paul Revere also used a secret code with lantern signals—one if by land, two if by sea. Here are some other ways to send secret messages:

Picket Fence Cipher: Count the number of letters in your message. If there is an odd number, add a dummy letter to the end. Now write the message on two lines, with every other letter on the lower line.

For example, the message "I have ten cats" would be written

```
I     A     E     E     C     T
   H     V     T     N     A     S
```

Write the top line then the bottom line: I A E E C T H V T N A S.

You can use a "fence" that is three or four letters high to make the message harder to decipher.

Pigpen Cipher: Draw two tic-tac-toe boards and two large *X*s. Put dots in the second tic-tac-toe board and the second *X*. In each space created by the shapes, put a letter. Here is one possible way to arrange the letters.

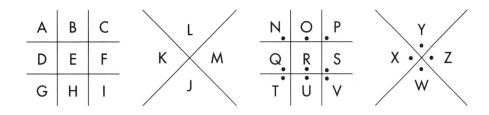

To create a message, draw the shape instead of the letter in the message. For example, the message "Hello" would become ⊓ ☐ ∨ ∨ ⊔

Newspaper Code: This type of code was used many years ago in England. Take a page from a newspaper. Starting from a preselected spot (top-left column and down or bottom right column and up, for example), put a pin prick under letters (or words) that spell out your message. To read the message, hold the newspaper up to the light to see which letters are marked.

Use one of these ciphers or create your own and write a message to a friend.

MODULAR ARITHMETIC **27**

Numerical Enciphering

1. Alberti made his enciphering machine using letters. It is common in *cryptography* (the study and practice of making messages secret) to assign the following numerical values to each letter in the alphabet: A = 1, B = 2, C = 3, . . . , Z = 26. Write the numerical value for each letter below and also on your enciphering machine.

2. What is the numerical value of Y?

3. What is the Caesar Cipher equivalent of Y?

4. What is the numerical value for the Caesar Cipher equivalent of Y?

5. In Activity 1, you learned one way to write a rule for a Caesar Cipher: *P* + 3 → *C*. Write a numerical rule for the Caesar Cipher that takes into account what happens to Y.

6. Write a numerical rule with regard to Y for an additive shift of 12.

7. Give an example of a common use of an additive shift 12. It need not be related to a code.

8. Do you know a mathematical convention for writing a numerical shift such as the ones above? Discuss with your group. Make an educated guess, and write it down. Then read the Interest Link "Modular Arithmetic."

Mod Arithmetic

1. A mathematical rule for the numerical equivalent of the Caesar Cipher (shift 3) could be written as follows:

   $C \equiv P + 3$ mod 26, where P is the numerical value for any letter in the plaintext and C is its equivalent in the ciphertext. The symbol $\equiv$ means congruence. For example, we know that $2 \neq 28$, but $2 \equiv 28$ mod 26. In mod 26, 2 and 28 have equivalent values.

   The interpretation of this rule, $C \equiv P + 3$ mod 26, is exactly what you have been doing.

Modular Addition	$C \equiv P + 3$ mod 26
Take any number P	for example $P = 25$
add 3 to it	$25 + 3 = 28$
subtract 26 (mod value) until the difference is between 1 and 26	$28 - 26 = 2$
$C =$ the difference	$C = 2$

   You have probably heard many names for modular arithmetic, such as *clock arithmetic, remainder arithmetic, modular arithmetic,* and *modulus arithmetic.* They are all perfectly valid labels. In this module, we are going to use the term *modular arithmetic,* or sometimes *mod arithmetic* for short.

2. How many different values are there for C in mod 26? List them.

3. How many different values are there for C in mod 7? List them.

Mod Arithmetic

4. Determine C in each of the following number sentences.

   a. $C \equiv 6 + 3 \bmod 7$ b. $C \equiv 2 + 3 \bmod 7$

   c. $C \equiv 6 + 1 \bmod 7$ d. $C \equiv 6 + 6 \bmod 7$

5. Find five different pairs (a, b) that satisfy the number sentence $a + b \bmod 7 \equiv 4$.

6. Make an addition table mod 7. Write it in the grid below.

Addition Mod 7

+	1	2	3	4	5	6	7	8	9	10
1										
2										
3										
4										
5										
6										
7										
8										
9										
10										

7. As a group, analyze the addition mod 7 table. Record your observations.

Mod Arithmetic

8. Are any of the rows and columns in this table repeats? If you crossed out any repetitive rows or columns, would you lose any information? Explain.

9. In regular addition, 0 is the additive identity (the identity element with respect to addition). Explain what that means. If you do not know the term *additive identity,* research it.

10. Are there any 0s in your addition mod 7 table? Is there any number than acts as an additive identity? If so, what is it? Give an example to support your response.

11. Complete the addition mod 7 table.

Addition Mod 7

+	1	2	3	4	5	6	7
1							
2							
3							
4							
5							
6							
7							

12. Is the table in question 11 a complete mod 7 addition table? Explain.

Mod Arithmetic

13. What is an additive inverse? Research it, if necessary.

14. Discuss with your group what the additive inverse for 3 mod 7 would be. Record your conclusion and explain your thinking.

15. List the additive inverse for each number.

16. Subtraction is the inverse of addition: $2 - 4 \mod 7 \equiv ?$ and $4 + ? \mod 7 \equiv 2$. Discuss with your group how you would use the addition mod 7 table to do subtraction mod 7. Explain, giving an example to illustrate.

17. What is $3 - 6 \mod 7$? Explain your procedure and give another example to illustrate it.

Multiplication Mod 7

1. Using what you know about the formula for modular addition, what do you think 6 × 4 mod 7 is? Explain, and give another example to illustrate.

2. Determine C in each of the following number sentences.

   a. $C \equiv 5 \times 3 \mod 7$ b. $C \equiv 2 \times 3 \mod 7$

   c. $C \equiv 6 \times 4 \mod 7$ d. $C \equiv 6 \times 6 \mod 7$

3. List 5 different pairs (a, b) that satisfy the number sentence $a \times b \mod 7 \equiv 4$.

4. Make a multiplication table mod 7. Write it in the grid below.

Multiplication Mod 7

×							

5. As a group, analyze the multiplication mod 7 table. Record your observations.

Multiplication Mod 7

6. In regular arithmetic, what is the *multiplicative identity* (the identity element with respect to multiplication)? Explain.

7. What is the multiplicative identity mod 7? Give an example to illustrate.

8. What is a *multiplicative inverse*? Research it, if necessary.

9. List the multiplicative inverse for each number in mod 7.

10. Division is the inverse of multiplication: $2 \div 4 \mod 7 \equiv ?$ and $4 \times ? \mod 7 \equiv 2$. Discuss with your group how you would use the multiplication mod 7 table to do division mod 7. Explain, giving an example to illustrate.

11. What is $5 \div 4 \mod 7$? Explain your procedure, and give another example to illustrate it.

Mod Arithmetic Revisited

1. What is the *commutative property of addition*? Explain, and give an example to illustrate.

2. Is addition mod 7 commutative? Explain, and give an example to illustrate.

3. What is the *associative property of addition*? Explain, and give an example to illustrate.

4. Is addition mod 7 associative? Explain, and give an example to illustrate.

5. Is addition in any mod arithmetic commutative and associative? Explain, and give examples to illustrate.

Mod Arithmetic Revisited

6. What is the *commutative property of multiplication*? Explain, and give an example to illustrate.

7. Is multiplication mod 7 commutative? Explain, and give an example to illustrate.

8. What is the *associative property of multiplication*? Explain, and give an example to illustrate.

9. Is multiplication mod 7 associative? Explain, and give an example to illustrate.

10. Is multiplication in any mod arithmetic commutative and associative? Explain, and give examples to illustrate.

Mod 4, 6, 8: What Do Spies Appreciate?

1. What is special about the number 7? Discuss as a group, and explain your conclusions.

2. How does the number 7 differ from 4, 6, or 8? Discuss as a group, and explain your conclusions.

3. Make a multiplication table mod 4, 6, or 8. You choose which of these mods you want to investigate. Write it in the grid below.

Multiplication Mod _____

×								

4. Analyze the multiplication mod _____ table. Compare it to the multiplication mod 7 table. Record your observations.

Mod 4, 6, 8: What Do Spies Appreciate?

5. What is the multiplicative identity mod _____? Explain.

6. Does every number have an multiplicative inverse? Explain.

7. What is 2 ÷ 2 mod 4 (or 6, or 8)?

8. Can you be sure what 2 ÷ 2 mod 4 (or 6, or 8) is?

9. Which mod do you prefer? Explain.

10. Which mod would a spy prefer? Explain.

ACTIVITY
3

MULTIPLICATIVE SHIFTS

Overview

Students learn how to do modular multiplication on a calculator. They use this skill to explore multiplicative shifts. They discover that there are a limited number of multiplicative shifts that result in a one-to-one correspondence between the plaintext and the ciphertext. They also learn that the basis of determining which shifts are usable for coding lies in relatively prime numbers.

Time. One to two 45-minute periods.

Purpose. As students continue to learn of the significance of mathematics in developing cryptosystems, they hone their operational and logic skills developing a system to do modular multiplication on the calculator.

Materials. *For the teacher:*

◆ Transparencies of Student Sheets 3.1–3.4

For each student:

◆ Student Sheets 3.1–3.4
◆ The Alberti Enciphering Machine (from Activity 1)
◆ Calculator

Getting Ready

1. Duplicate Student Sheets 3.1–3.4.
2. Locate enciphering machines and calculators.
3. Prepare transparencies of Student Sheets 3.1–3.4.

Background Information

In this activity, students learn how to do modular multiplication on a calculator. They use this skill to explore multiplicative shifts. Recall that additive shifts are of the form $C \equiv P + k$ mod 26, where k is an integer. Multiplicative shifts are of the form $C \equiv k \times P$ mod 26, where k is a positive integer. In reality, additive and multiplicative shifts do not need to be mod 26. But in this activity, we use only mod 26. If the plaintext were to include the 26 letters of the alphabet plus some punctuation, such as a comma, a period, and a space, then the additive and multiplicative shifts would need to be mod 29.

On Student Sheet 3.1, students use their enciphering machines to decode messages that lead them to investigate additive and multiplicative shifts. Students realize the Alberti Enciphering Machine is mod 26 and there are 26 additive shifts. The last question instructs students to develop a method for performing modular multiplication on a calculator.

Student Sheet 3.2 illustrates an efficient method of performing modular multiplication on a calculator. The method is outlined for the example 11×25 mod 26.

Problem	Step	Calculation
11 × 25 mod 26	1. Multiply numbers.	11 × 25 = 275
	2. Divide by mod value.	275 ÷ 26 = 10.57692308
	3. Subtract integral part.	10.57692308 − 10 = 0.57692308
	4. Multiply by mod value.	0.57692308 × 26 = 15

Therefore, 11×25 mod $26 \equiv 15$.

Student Sheet 3.3 formally introduces multiplicative shifts. Students are given the general form $C \equiv k \times P$ mod 26 and a ciphertext to decode. The primary task is to determine the value of k (the key) for this multiplicative shift.

Not all multiplicative shifts are used in cryptography. Some multiplicative shifts do not result in a one-to-one correspondence between plaintext and ciphertext. Look at the following table for example in which $k = 2$:

$$C \equiv 2 \times P \bmod 26$$

	A	B	C	D	E	F	G	H	I	J	K	L	M
P	1	2	3	4	5	6	7	8	9	10	11	12	13
C	2	4	6	8	10	12	14	16	18	20	22	24	26

	N	O	P	Q	R	S	T	U	V	W	X	Y	Z
P	14	15	16	17	18	19	20	21	22	23	24	25	26
C	2	4	6	8	10	12	14	16	18	20	22	24	26

$C \equiv 2 \times P \bmod 26$, takes both D $\rightarrow$ 8 and Q $\rightarrow$ 8. Even if the cryptanalyst knew the key, she would not know the plaintext value of a ciphertext 8; it could be D or Q.

Numbers that are relatively prime to 26, numbers that have no common factor with 26 (3, 5, 7, 9, 11, 15, 17, 19, 21, 23, and 25), are keys that yield multiplicative shifts that result in *monoalphabetic ciphers,* ciphers that are in one-to-one correspondence with the plaintext.

$$C \equiv 9 \times P \bmod 26$$

	A	B	C	D	E	F	G	H	I	J	K	L	M
P	1	2	3	4	5	6	7	8	9	10	11	12	13
C	9	18	1	10	19	2	11	20	3	12	21	4	13

	N	O	P	Q	R	S	T	U	V	W	X	Y	Z
P	14	15	16	17	18	19	20	21	22	23	24	25	26
C	22	5	14	23	6	15	24	7	16	25	8	17	0

Note that 26 (mod base) is not prime, yet the result is a monoalphabetic cipher. The criterion for a monoalphabetic cipher is that k be relatively prime to the mod value. There is, of course, the additional cipher when $k = 1$, which is monoalphabetic, but it is never used in cryptology.

On Student Sheet 3.4, students decode ciphertexts that have been encoded with various multiplicative shifts. The ciphertext also leads students to explore multiplicative shifts in general. All the ciphertexts focus on discovering the fact that when k is relatively prime to 26, the resulting ciphertext is monoalphabetic.

The Career Link "Cryptographic Technician" and the Writing Link "The Golden Bug" may be used at any time during this unit to further student interest.

Presenting the Activity

The Alberti Machine Revisited. Assign students to groups of two, three, or four students. Hand out Student Sheet 3.1 and let groups experience deciphering numeric ciphertext using their enciphering machines. As you circulate among groups, make sure all students understand there are 26 different additive shifts on the Alberti Enciphering Machine. Discuss why only 25 are used in cryptography.

After students have completed question 4, have the class share ideas on multiplicative shifts, including numeric rules. This discussion will provide you with a picture of their thinking, not only on multiplicative shifts, but also on their abilities to extend ideas and concepts—in particular their abilities to generalize from additive shifts to multiplicative shifts and their abilities to symbolize the generalization.

After students have completed question 5, have another class discussion to allow students to share their methods for performing modular multiplication on a calculator. Accept all accurate methods, and emphasize the numerous processes. Do not worry about efficiency and elegance, but rather encourage exploration. Use a transparency of Student Sheet 3.1 to write out the plaintext in questions 1–3 and to explore students' ideas for questions 4 and 5.

Mod Multiplication on a Calculator. Hand out Student Sheet 3.2 and allow time for groups to discuss the example. Circulate among them to make sure all students understand the process. Work through a few examples as a class on an overhead transparency, if necessary. After the work is done, discuss as a class the strategies and variations. Students could very likely derive an even more efficient method.

Multiplicative Shifts. Hand out Student Sheet 3.3. As groups work, observe their strategies to decode the ciphertext. Once students hypothesize which ciphertext letter corresponds to plaintext E, observe the strategies used to determine $k = 3$.

$$k = \underline{\quad 3 \quad}$$

	A	B	C	D	E	F	G	H	I	J	K	L	M
P	1	2	3	4	5	6	7	8	9	10	11	12	13
C	3	6	9	12	15	18	21	24	1	4	7	10	13

	N	O	P	Q	R	S	T	U	V	W	X	Y	Z
P	14	15	16	17	18	19	20	21	22	23	24	25	26
C	16	19	22	25	2	5	8	11	14	17	20	23	26

As groups discuss question 3, circulate among them to ensure that all students see the pattern in the cipher table—the next letter in the ciphertext has a value of three more than the value of the preceding letter. Ask students how they might use this knowledge to quickly create a cipher table for any known k. Use a transparency of Student Sheet 3.3 for discussions.

After students have completed the work, have a discussion focused on the ease of creating ciphertext once the key is known (a process that is used among cryptographers) and one that could be used among friends. Contrast this process to that of cryptanalysis, the deciphering of codes for which the key is unknown. Elicit students' ideas regarding the security of multiplicative shifts in both types of situations.

More About Multiplicative Shifts. Hand out Student Sheet 3.4. If students seem frustrated, give another hint or clue as to the value of k, such as k is prime and it is greater than 10.

After the work is completed, discuss multiplicative shifts. Compare them to additive shifts in preparation for the next type cipher. Activity 5 focuses on affine ciphers, which are of the form $C \equiv a \times P + b \bmod 26$, where a is a positive integer greater than zero and b is any integer. Note that affine ciphers are a combination of additive and multiplicative shifts. When $a = 1$, the affine cipher reduces to an additive shift, and when $b = 0$, it reduces to a multiplicative shift.

Revisit the issue of security at some point in the discussion. Ciphers, particularly affine, are significantly more difficult to decode if the key is not known. This could be frustrating to some students, but that is what makes these ciphers good secret codes. Throughout the module, point out this contrast: when you know the key, ciphers are easy to break; when you do not know the key, some are difficult to break.

Discussion Questions

1. What is the difference between the algorithm (the rule) and the key?

2. What would an enciphering machine for a multiplicative shift look like?

3. How would you use a calculator to do mod 7 multiplication?

4. Compare the ease in using codes in which the key is known to the difficulty of breaking codes for which the key in not known. Discuss these situations in terms of security of ciphertext.

Assessment Questions

1. Natasha has decided to use a multiplicative shift in her communications with Boris. They are still using a plaintext alphabet of 26 letters plus a comma, a period, and a space.

   a. Give the numeric rule you think they are using.

   b. Dudley intercepted a message, and he came to you to decode it. Write the ciphertext and the plaintext.

2. Describe the steps you would use in creating the cipher table for Natasha's key. Give a detailed example of how you would determine the ciphertext equivalent of N.

3. As a group, decide on the plaintext alphabet (plus symbols) and which key you will use among yourselves to send ciphertext created by a multiplicative shift.

   a. Give the numeric rule for your shift.

   b. Give the cipher table for your shift.

   c. Compose a message and write the ciphertext.

4. Exchange ciphertexts with another group and give them the general rule, but not the key.

   a. Decode the received ciphertext.

   b. Give the key they used.

   c. Write both the ciphertext and the plaintext.

Cryptographic Technician

Secret messages are not limited to spies with secret compartments in suitcases and microfilmed code books. Cryptographic technicians deal with coded messages every day in their careers. They use computers and decoding machinery to encode, send, and decode messages.

Most cryptographic technicians work for the government, including the military, the National Security Agency, and other intelligence operations. They are responsible for sending and receiving information that needs to be kept secret. Because of this, the government investigates a person's background before hiring him or her as a cryptographic technician.

One example of the important role of cryptographic technicians is in the U.S. Armed Forces. When military personnel are away on assignments, they receive orders over radio waves, telephone, or computer. Because others can intercept these messages, they are sent in secret code. Cryptographic technicians receive the messages and feed them into a decoding machine to help them create decoded messages. To send messages, they must select the code and type the messages into special machinery that encodes the messages.

Cryptographic technicians also work for private companies that need to keep information secret, especially if it is on computer. For example, banks often use secret codes to transfer funds from one bank to another by computer.

To become a cryptographic technician, you need a high school degree plus several months to two years of special training. The armed forces and some businesses will give you this special training if you decide to become a cryptographic technician for them.

The Golden Bug

Edgar Allen Poe was not only an author, he was also an amateur cryptographer. He once challenged readers of his newspaper column to try to stump him with their coded messages. He was able to decipher just about every one of them.

In his story *The Golden Bug,* Poe uses a cryptogram in the plot. A *cryptogram* is a message in code or cipher. In the story, a man finds an unusual gold-colored beetle and sketches it on a sheet of paper he found on the beach. When his friend holds the paper up to a fire to see the picture, a message written in invisible ink appears. The message is in code, which the two men must decipher.

Read *The Golden Bug* to discover the meaning of the message. Then write your own story involving a coded secret message. Let your readers try to figure out the mystery message first, but be sure to reveal the secret by the end of the story!

The Alberti Machine Revisited

Each ciphertext has been encoded using the Alberti Enciphering Machine.
Decode and respond in plaintext.

1. H S L E   X Z O   O Z P D   E S P   L W M P C E T   X L N S T Y P   F D P ?

2. O V D   T H U F   K P M M L Y L U A   H K K P A P C L   Z O P M A Z

   H Y L   W V Z Z P I S L   V U   H U   H S I L Y A P   T H J O P U L ?

3. V Q H S D   S G D   M T L D Q H B   Q T K D   E N Q   S G H R

   Z C C H S H U D   R G H E S .

4. H I W G V M F I   E   Q Y P X M T P M G E X M Z I   W L M J X   E R H

   A V M X I   E   V Y P I .

5. J V G U   L B H E   T E B H C   Q R G R E Z V A R   U B J   G B

   Q B   Z B Q   Z H Y G V C Y V P N G V B A   B A   G U R

   P N Y P H Y N G B E .   B H G Y V A R   G U R   F G R C F

   V A   C Y N V A G R K G .

Mod Multiplication on a Calculator

1. One efficient method to perform modular multiplication on a calculator is shown here:

Problem	Step	Calculation
11 × 25 mod 26	1. Multiply numbers.	11 × 25 = 275
	2. Divide by mod value.	275 ÷ 26 = 10.57692308
	3. Subtract integral part.	10.57692308 − 10 = 0.57692308
	4. Multiply by mod value.	0.57692308 × 26 = 15

Therefore, 11 × 25 mod 26 ≡ 15.

2. Discuss with your group why this works. Explain.

3. Practice modular multiplication on the calculator.

   a. 7 × 23 mod 26 ≡   b. 5 × 17 mod 26 ≡

   c. 11 × 25 mod 23 ≡   d. 11 × 25 mod 29 ≡

4. Compose and solve two modular multiplication problems on the calculator.
   a.   b.

5. What is 6 × 26 mod 26?

Multiplicative Shifts

1. A multiplicative shift is of the form $C \equiv k \times P \bmod 26$, where k is a positive integer. The ciphertext given below has been encoded with a multiplicative shift mod 26. The following numerical values were assigned to the plaintext. Hint: $k < 10$.

	A	B	C	D	E	F	G	H	I	J	K	L	M
P	1	2	3	4	5	6	7	8	9	10	11	12	13

	N	O	P	Q	R	S	T	U	V	W	X	Y	Z
P	14	15	16	17	18	19	20	21	22	23	24	25	26

Decode the ciphertext and respond in plaintext.

Q X C H   A E   G   A P   H X A E   M K J H A V J A I C H A N O   E X A R H ?

2. Complete the cipher table for the above multiplicative shift.

$k =$ _____

	A	B	C	D	E	F	G	H	I	J	K	L	M
P	1	2	3	4	5	6	7	8	9	10	11	12	13
C													

	N	O	P	Q	R	S	T	U	V	W	X	Y	Z
P	14	15	16	17	18	19	20	21	22	23	24	25	26
C													

Multiplicative Shifts

3. Discuss any patterns you observe in the cipher table. Report your conclusions.

4. Some multiplicative shifts are better than others. As a group, explore the following multiplicative shifts:

   a. $C \equiv 4 \times P \bmod 26$

$k =$ _____

	A	B	C	D	E	F	G	H	I	J	K	L	M
C													

	N	O	P	Q	R	S	T	U	V	W	X	Y	Z
C													

   b. $C \equiv 5 \times P \bmod 26$

$k =$ _____

	A	B	C	D	E	F	G	H	I	J	K	L	M
C													

	N	O	P	Q	R	S	T	U	V	W	X	Y	Z
C													

Multiplicative Shifts

c. $C \equiv 6 \times P \bmod 26$

k = _____

	A	B	C	D	E	F	G	H	I	J	K	L	M
C													

	N	O	P	Q	R	S	T	U	V	W	X	Y	Z
C													

d. $C \equiv 7 \times P \bmod 26$

k = _____

	A	B	C	D	E	F	G	H	I	J	K	L	M
C													

	N	O	P	Q	R	S	T	U	V	W	X	Y	Z
C													

5. Which of the above multiplicative shifts would you prefer to use? Explain.

More About Multiplicative Shifts

The ciphertexts given below have been encoded with mod 26 multiplicative shifts. The standard numerical coding has been used for the plaintext: A = 1, B = 2, and so on. Decode the ciphertexts and respond in plaintext. Hint: *k* is always prime.

1. JIS MKXO MIR DDHU MWBLUTBUGKLUHC

   AJUNL GUTJCPA KPC LJCPC?

2. JIS MKXO MIR DDHU MWBLUTBUGKLUHC

   AJUNLA YUHC IXC LI IXC LPKXABKLUIXA?

   XKMC LJCM.

3. EDGJ BA SAQ TAJKUI GNAQJ JDI MAB

   LLXK MQFJKHFKUGJKXI CDKPJC JDGJ

   VICQFJ KT ATI JA ATI JVGTCFGJKATC?

More About Multiplicative Shifts

4. DAE MGTS UKHDIV JGNFIC EAQFB SAQ

    DGXI JA MGYI KT AVBIV JA BIUABI GTS

    MAB LLXK MQFJKHFKUGJKXI CDKPJ UKHDIV?

5. VYU WQEIDQ SDQ MITPORTOESPOBQ WVOJP

    EORVQDW?

    (Hint: An A in ciphertext would be a K in plaintext: K → A.)

ACTIVITY
4

PRIME
NUMBERS

Overview

Students search for all the prime numbers between 1 and 100. Using square tiles, they form all the unique rectangles they can that have an area of n square units, for $n = 1, 2, \ldots, 100$. They also determine the factors for each n and then explore the relationship between the number of unique rectangles, the dimensions of the unique rectangles, and the factors. They determine which numbers are prime and which are composite, after which they explore the prime sieve, another method to identify the primes between 1 and 100.

Time. One 45-minute period.

Purpose. Students develop a more solid understanding of prime numbers as they explore the concept from multiple perspectives.

Materials. *For the teacher:*

◆ Transparencies of Student Sheets 4.1–4.3

For each student:

◆ Student Sheets 4.1–4.3
◆ Calculator

For each group of students:

◆ 100 square tiles

Getting Ready

1. Duplicate Student Sheets 4.1–4.3.
2. Locate square tiles.
3. Prepare transparencies of Student Sheets 4.1–4.3.

Background Information

This activity is an in-depth exploration of prime numbers. On Student Sheets 4.1 and 4.2, students connect a graphical representation of factors to the familiar symbolic one. Using square tiles, students form all the unique rectangles they can that have an area of *n* square units for *n* = 1, 2, . . . , 100.

For example, when *n* = 1, there is only one unique rectangle, actually a square, that can be formed. Its dimensions are 1 unit × 1 unit.

When *n* = 2, there is only one unique rectangle. Note that a 90° rotation of this rectangle is congruent to the rectangle, and therefore, it would not be considered a different rectangle. The dimensions of this rectangle are 1 unit × 2 units.

When *n* = 3, there is only one unique rectangle. Its dimensions are 1 unit × 3 units.

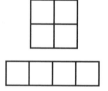

When *n* = 4, there are two unique rectangles. The dimensions of one are 2 units × 2 units, and the dimensions of the other are 1 unit × 4 units.

The number 1 is special and can only be represented by a square. Note that those numbers for which there is only one unique rectangle that is not a square are prime, and their factors are in one-to-one correspondence with their dimensions. The composite numbers can be represented by more than one rectangle, and the dimensions of all the representations are in one-to-one correspondence with its factors. For example, the factors of 4 are 1, 2, and 4, which are the dimensions of the two rectangles.

Student Sheet 4.3 introduces students to a clever way to identify all the primes between 1 and 103. Students follow these directions to determine all the prime numbers between 1 and 103:

a. Circle all the primes in the first row (2, 3, 5, and 7 are prime).

b. Draw a line through the first column (except for the 2) and through the entire third and fifth columns (all the multiples of 2).

c. Draw a line through the second column (except for the 3) (all the multiples of 3).

d. Draw a diagonal line down and to the left (/) between the 5 in the top row (but not actually through the 5 itself) and the first 5 in the left column. Draw parallel diagonal lines between pairs of 5s in the side columns (all the multiples of 5).

e. Draw a diagonal line down and to the right (\) between the first 7 in the left column and the first 7 in the right column. Do this again for the second 7s (all the multiples of 7).

f. Circle any number that does not have a line through it (all are prime!).

This is what students should end up with.

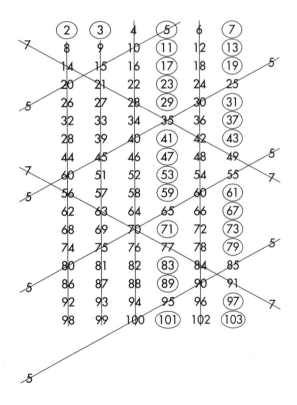

The largest square in the table is 100, the square root of which is 10. The largest prime factor for any number in this table is 7, the greatest prime less than 10. If you eliminate all the multiples of the primes less than or equal to 7, you have eliminated all the composite numbers. You are left with just the primes. Students like this trick, and it facilitates their understanding of factors and primes.

The Career Link "Elizebeth Friedman" may be used at any time during the activity to further student interest.

Presenting the Activity

Prime Time. Divide students into working groups of two, three, or four students. Give each group about 100 square tiles or enough that each student can work with the tiles. Students like to manipulate the tiles themselves, not watch others do it. Then they can compare their results with those of all the group members.

Hand out Student Sheet 4.1. Circulate among groups to make sure students are making the connection between the dimensions of the rectangles and the factors. When all the groups have completed the work at least through $n = 10$, have a class discussion on congruent rectangles, unique rectangles, factors, and the relationship between the dimensions of the rectangles and factors. Use a transparency of Student Sheet 4.1 if needed.

After students have finished, ask them to share their definitions of prime and composite numbers. The discussion of whether or not 1 is prime is usually interesting. Students have excellent reasons to support the arguments for and against. Mathematically, it is defined as a special number, not a prime number. The uniqueness of 1 in this activity is that it is the only number for which there is only one unique rectangle that is a square. A square is a special case of a rectangle, so 1 is special in this sense. Elicit this fact, and use it in support of the definition that 1 is a special number.

Primes Unlimited. Hand out Student Sheet 4.2, which continues the work of relating dimensions and factors for $n = 100$. Allow students access to the tiles, but do not insist that they make every rectangle once they are able to generalize the process and work at the symbolic level. To make sure students understand the process, visit each group, and have each student use the tiles to show all the rectangles for a number between 30 and 100. After groups discuss questions 4 and 5, use a transparency of Student Sheet 4.2 to fill out the table. Use students' numbers and have them share their methods of determining whether a number has a factor or is prime.

Prime Sieve. Hand out Student Sheet 4.3. After groups discuss why you are left with just prime numbers, have them share their ideas with the class. Ask why we do not need to consider multiples of primes greater than 7. Use a transparency of Student Sheet 4.2 if needed.

At some point, discuss making a prime sieve for the numbers 1 to 200. Ask students:

- What would such a sieve look like?

- How would it differ from the sieve for 1 to 103?

- What prime factors would you need to consider?

Students might immediately think you would need to consider factors up to 20—since you have doubled the number of integers ($200 = 2 \times 100$), you would have to check on primes up to double the number checked for the first sieve ($20 = 2 \times 10$). The square root of $200 = 14.14$, so you only need to consider primes up to 13. This is a good activity for middle school students, many of whom do not yet have a thorough understanding of exponential functions.

Discussion Questions

1. If you did not recognize congruent rectangles as different representations of the same rectangle, how many rectangles are there for $n = 5$?

2. Why do mathematicians put so much focus on prime numbers?

3. Cryptographers also put much emphasis on prime numbers. Why do you think they do so?

4. How many primes are between 1 and 100? How many primes do you think are between 100 and 200?

Assessment Questions

1. As a group, design a prime sieve to determine the primes between 1 and 200. Draw it and give the rules on how to use it.

2. Add the ages of all members in your class. Call it a. Determine if $a - 1$ is prime. Support your conclusion in writing.

3. Write a paragraph describing the difference between primes and composites in terms that a nonscientifically trained parent could understand.

Elizebeth Friedman

Elizebeth Friedman was a famous cryptanalyst who deciphered the secret codes of smugglers and bootleggers in the early 1900s. She began her career working for a wealthy merchant, George Fabyan, who was trying to prove that encrypted in Shakespeare's works was the name of the real author, whom Fabyan believed was Sir Francis Bacon.

It was there that she met her husband William, a geneticist and fellow cryptanalyst. The two went on to become the world's best cryptanalysis pair.

In the 1930s, Friedman was a valuable resource for the U.S. Coast Guard as she deciphered messages between criminal organizations trying to smuggle liquor into the United States. (The Prohibition outlawed liquor at that time.)

This was a very difficult task because the smugglers used professional cryptographers to encode sophisticated ciphertext. Friedman studied hundreds of codes and made many trial-and-error attempts before she succeeded in breaking the code. Later, she used her skills on intercepted messages from other smuggling operations. Her triumphs resulted in a big loss for criminals, including the Ezra brothers' drug ring in San Francisco and the Lim opium ring in Canada.

Friedman ended her career as she began it—studying Shakespeare. She and her husband wrote *The Shakespearean Ciphers Examined*—their proof that Sir Francis Bacon could not have authored the famous Shakespearean plays.

UPI/Corbis-Bettman

Prime Time

1. Take one tile. Convince yourself that you can make only one rectangle using one tile. Sketch the rectangle below.

   What are the dimensions of the rectangle?

2. Take two tiles. Determine how many unique rectangles you can make with the two tiles. Sketch them below.

3. If a rectangle can be made to fit exactly on top of another rectangle, the two rectangles are said to be *congruent*. They are considered to be the same, they are not unique. With this note, examine your conclusions in 2. How many unique rectangles can you make with two square tiles?

4. What is a factor? What are the factors of 2? What is the relationship between the factors of 2 and the dimensions of the rectangles made with two tiles?

5. Continuing in this manner, determine how many unique rectangles you can make with three tiles, four tiles, and so on. For each number of tiles, record in the table on the next page the number of unique rectangles, the dimensions of each rectangle, and the factors of each number.

Prime Time

Number of Tiles	Number of Unique Rectangles	Dimensions of Each Rectangle	Factors	
1	1			
2				
3				
4				
5				
6				
7				
8				
9				
10				
11				
12				
13				
14				
15				
16				
17				
18				
19				
20				

Prime Time

6. As a group, examine the table. What is the relationship between number of rectangles, dimensions of rectangles, and factors? Explain.

7. What is a prime number? If you are not certain, research it. As a group, write a definition of a prime number.

8. What is a composite number? If you are not certain, research it. As a group, write a definition of a composite number.

9. Label the last column in your table "Prime." Determine which numbers are prime and which numbers are composite. Put a *P* in the Prime column for each prime number and a *C* for each composite.

10. Is 1 prime? Explain.

Primes Unlimited

1. Complete the tables on this page and the next page.

Num.	Num. of Rect.	Dimensions or Factors	Prime	Num.	Num. of Rect.	Dimensions or Factors	Prime
21				41			
22				42			
23				43			
24				44			
25				45			
26				46			
27				47			
28				48			
29				49			
30				50			
31				51			
32				52			
33				53			
34				54			
35				55			
36				56			
37				57			
38				58			
39				59			
40				60			

Primes Unlimited

Num.	Num. of Rect.	Dimensions or Factors	Prime	Num.	Num. of Rect.	Dimensions or Factors	Prime
61				81			
62				82			
63				83			
64				84			
65				85			
66				86			
67				87			
68				88			
69				89			
70				90			
71				91			
72				92			
73				93			
74				94			
75				95			
76				96			
77				97			
78				98			
79				99			
80				100			

Primes Unlimited

2. How many prime numbers are there between 1 and 100? List them.

3. Is 101 prime? Explain.

4. Do you know any quick checks to determine if a number is prime? List at least three quick checks. If you do not readily come up with three checks, research it.

5. Use your quick checks to determine if any numbers between 102 and 110 are prime. List any primes you find.

Prime Sieve

1. Follow the directions to find all the prime numbers between 1 and 103.
   a. Circle all the primes in the first row.
   b. Draw a line through the first column (except for the 2) and through the entire third and fifth columns.
   c. Draw a line through the second column (except for the 3).
   d. Draw a diagonal line down and to the left (/) between 5 in the top row (but not actually through the 5 itself) and the first 5 in the left column. Draw parallel diagonal lines between pairs of 5s in the side columns.
   e. Draw a diagonal line down and to the right (\) between the first 7 in the left column and the first 7 in the right column. Do this again for the second 7s.
   f. Circle any number that does not have a line through it.

Side Column	First	Second	Third	Fourth	Fifth	Sixth	Side Column
	2	3	4	5	6	7	
7	8	9	10	11	12	13	
	14	15	16	17	18	19	5
	20	21	22	23	24	25	
5	26	27	28	29	30	31	
	32	33	34	35	36	37	
	28	39	40	41	42	43	
	44	45	46	47	48	49	5
7	60	51	52	53	54	55	7
5	56	57	58	59	60	61	
	62	63	64	65	66	67	
	68	69	70	71	72	73	
	74	75	76	77	78	79	5
	80	81	82	83	84	85	
5	86	87	88	89	90	91	
	92	93	94	95	96	97	7
	98	99	100	101	102	103	

5

2. Explain why you are left with just the primes.

ACTIVITY
5

AFFINE CIPHERS

Overview

Students discover that affine ciphers are a combination of additive and multiplicative ciphers resulting in the form $C \equiv a \times P + b \bmod d$. They learn that while it is easy to encode affine ciphers, they are difficult to decode if you do not know the key. Affine ciphers prove to be quite secure for most middle schoolers—most of their friends and family cannot break these ciphers unless they know how to apply some algebra. Students are introduced to a method of solving two equations in two unknowns as a technique to decode affine ciphers.

Time. Two to three 45-minute periods.

Purpose. Students learn that seemingly unbreakable codes can be broken with a little knowledge of algebra. For many students, this exercise will give more importance to algebra and reasons for studying it.

Materials. *For the teacher:*

◆ Transparencies of Student Sheets 5.1–5.3

For each student:

◆ Student Sheets 5.1–5.3
◆ Calculator

For each group of students:

◆ Mathematics reference book

Getting Ready

1. Duplicate Student Sheets 5.1–5.3.
2. Locate calculators and mathematics reference books.
3. Prepare transparencies of Student Sheets 5.1–5.3.

Background Information

In this activity, students encounter a cryptosystem they can not easily break. Affine ciphers are a combination of additive and multiplicative ciphers of the form $C \equiv a \times P + b \mod d$ where a and b are positive integers and a is relatively prime to d. They learn that while it is easy to encode and decode affine ciphers if you know the key, it is quite difficult to decode them without the key. For example, if the key is (3, 2), then $C \equiv 3 \times P + 2 \mod 26$. We are again going to work with mod 26.

The plaintext numerical values are given by:

	A	B	C	D	E	F	G	H	I	J	K	L	M
P	1	2	3	4	5	6	7	8	9	10	11	12	13

	N	O	P	Q	R	S	T	U	V	W	X	Y	Z
P	14	15	16	17	18	19	20	21	22	23	24	25	26

If you know the key, for example (3, 2), it is quite easy to compute C. For $P = 1$, $C \equiv 3 \times P + 2 \mod 26 \equiv 3 \times 1 + 2 \mod 26 \equiv 5 \mod 26$. The ciphertext values for $C \equiv 3 \times P + 2 \mod 26$ are:

	A	B	C	D	E	F	G	H	I	J	K	L	M
C	5	8	11	14	17	20	23	26	3	6	9	12	15

	N	O	P	Q	R	S	T	U	V	W	X	Y	Z
C	18	21	24	27	4	7	10	13	16	19	22	25	2

If you do not know the key, the code is significantly more difficult to crack than either additive or multiplicative shifts.

For example, to decode the ciphertext given on Student Sheet 5.1: SZEJ DMLQ SEG MGQN JU QRKUNQ JZCG RUJQ?, count the frequency of the letters in the ciphertext to discover that Q is the most frequently used letter, occurring five times, and J is the next most frequently used, occurring four times. You could hypothesize that $Q \equiv E$ and $J \equiv T$. This would leave the translation as

C: SZEJ DMLQ SEG MGQN JU QRKUNQ JZCG RUJQ?

P: ...T ...E ... ..E. .. E....E T... ..TE?

There is no easy method to discern the pattern $3 \times P + 2 \mod 26$, and it is trial and error from here. You could determine the next most frequent letters, and refer to the frequency table given on Student Sheet 1.2.

Ciphertext Letter	Frequency in Ciphertext	Possible Letter in Plaintext
Q	5	E
J	4	T
G, U	3	A, O, I, N, S, H, R
S, Z, E, M, N, R	2	D, L, C, U
D, L, K, C	1	M, W, F, G, Y, P, B

Suppose $G \equiv A$ and $U \equiv O$. The plaintext becomes

C: SZEJ DMLQ SEG MGQN JU QRKUNQ JZCG RUJQ?

P: ...T ...E ..A .AE. TO E..O.E T..A .OTE?

The $U \equiv O$ looks plausible, but there are not many three-letter words ending in *a*. G most likely is not a vowel. Suppose $G \equiv N$, then the plaintext becomes

C: SZEJ DMLQ SEG MGQN JU QRKUNQ JZCG RUJQ?

P: ...T ...E ..N .NE. TO E..O.E T..N .OTE?

Not many four-letter words have NE in the middle. It could not be *ones*, because $U \equiv O$ and therefore, $M \neq O$. So, try $G \equiv S$.

C: SZEJ DMLQ SEG MGQN JU QRKUNQ JZCG RUJQ?

P: ...T ...E ..S .SE. TO E..O.E T..S .OTE?

Many three-lettered words end in *s* such as *has*, *was*, *tis* (but you already let $J \equiv T$, so *tis* is out!), *his*, and *yes* (but $Q \equiv E$, so *yes* is out). Let $E \equiv A$. The plaintext becomes

C: SZEJ DMLQ SEG MGQN JU QRKUNQ JZCG RUJQ?

P: ..AT ...E .AS .SE. TO E..O.E T..S .OTE?

This looks plausible. Let $S \equiv H$. The plaintext becomes

C: SZEJ DMLQ SEG MGQN JU QRKUNQ JZCG RUJQ?

P: H.AT ...E HAS .SE. TO E..O.E T..S .OTE?

The H.AT does not look good, so try $S \equiv W$. The plaintext becomes

C: SZEJ DMLQ SEG MGQN JU QRKUNQ JZCG RUJQ?

P: W.AT ...E WAS .SE. TO E..O.E T..S .OTE?

Aha! The first word is probably *what*, which means Z ≡ H. The plaintext becomes

    C: SZEJ DMLQ SEG MGQN JU QRKUNQ JZCG RUJQ?
    P: WHAT ...E WAS .SE. TO E..O.E TH.S .OTE?

The next to the last word is probably *this*, which means C ≡ I. The plaintext becomes

    C: SZEJ DMLQ SEG MGQN JU QRKUNQ JZCG RUJQ?
    P: WHAT ...E WAS .SE. TO E..O.E THIS .OTE?

The last word must be *note*, which means R ≡ N. The plaintext becomes

    C: SZEJ DMLQ SEG MGQN JU QRKUNQ JZCG RUJQ?
    P: WHAT ...E WAS .SE. TO EN.O.E THIS NOTE?

Note that there is still no easy method to discern the pattern $3 \times P + 2$. It is pure trial and error. At this stage, the frequencies do not really help. Knowledge of grammar and semantics is more useful.

There is an efficient strategy to decode affine ciphers, and it involves algebra. More specifically, it involves solving two equations in two unknowns—solving for *a* and *b*.

For example, in the ciphertext on Student Sheet 5.1, SZEJ DMLQ SEG MGQN JU QRKUNQ JZCG RUJQ, you can hypothesize that based on the frequency count, Q ≡ E and J ≡ T. Use algebra to determine the key. For example, in the algorithm $C \equiv a \times P + b \bmod 26$, hypothesizing that E → Q, you would substitute the numerical values for E (5) and Q (17) for the plaintext value *P* and the ciphertext value *C* in the rule for an affine cipher.

$$C \equiv a \times P + b \bmod 26$$
$$17 \equiv a \times 5 + b \bmod 26$$

Next, hypothesizing that T → J, you would substitute the numerical values T (20) and J (10) for the plaintext value *P* and the ciphertext value *C* in the algorithm for an affine cipher, resulting in a second equation.

$$10 \equiv a \times 20 + b \bmod 26$$

There are now two equations in two unknowns, *a* and *b*, which can be solved by graphing the two equations on the same set of coordinate axes.

$$17 \equiv a \times 5 + b \bmod 26$$
$$10 \equiv a \times 20 + b \bmod 26$$

Read Student Sheet 5.2 (page 83) to familiarize yourself with the steps students use to graph equivalent mod 26 equations.

- Students graph a series of equations which are equivalent in mod 26, for example, $17 \equiv a \times 5 + b \bmod 26$, $17 + 26 \equiv a \times 5 + b \bmod 26$ and, $17 + 52 \equiv a \times 5 + b \bmod 26$, and discover that they are parallel. They all have the same slope, but different intercepts.

- They repeat the process for equations that are equivalent to
  $10 \equiv a \times 20 + b \bmod 26$.

- The equations intersect in several places. Each line of one series intersects with each line of the other series, but only one point of intersection is a possible solution. The only point for which a and b are both positive integers is $(3, 2)$.

- For the above example, this leads to the enciphering rule
  $C \equiv 3 \times P + 2 \bmod 26$.

  Once you know the enciphering rule, you can use it to make a cipher table similar to the one given on page 72 giving the numerical value for each letter in the ciphertext. This table then could be used to decode the ciphertext.

  On Student Sheet 5.3, students exchange ciphertexts created with an affine cipher of their choice.

  The History Link "The War of Cryptographers" and the Writing Link "A Cryptic History" may be used at any time during this activity to further student interest.

Presenting the Activity

A Fine Cipher This Is. Divide students into small groups; four to a group works well for this activity so students can work in pairs but still have group discussions. As you create groups, keep in mind the fact that the material might prove difficult for some students.

Hand out Student Sheet 5.1 and allow time for each group to discuss the rule for an affine cipher. Make sure students understand what "*a* is relatively prime to *d*" means. Circulate among the groups to gauge how students are doing, keeping in mind that some groups might become frustrated with the process. You may want to have another class discussion on the security of affine ciphers, explaining that this is a fairly secure cipher and is much more difficult to break than additive and multiplicative shifts. However, with a little knowledge of algebra, the cipher can be broken.

Deciphering Affine Ciphers. Hand out Student Sheet 5.2 and explain that it introduces a method to determine the key to an affine cipher. Point out that the method is illustrated using the ciphertext given on Student Sheet 5.1. Explain that they are to go over the material in their groups to ensure everyone understands the method, and that you will be available to answer questions.

As you circulate among the groups, observe the scale students use on their coordinate grid. A uniform scale of one unit for each marker on both axes allows for very accurate drawing and should be encouraged. Be sure students extend each line to intersect both axes. They can tape grid pages together as needed. You might work with the class as a whole to go over the scale. Using an overhead transparency of the coordinate grid paper, elicit how to plot the first series of equivalent equations.

Have the students make the cipher table and decode the ciphertext in question 10. Orchestrate a class discussion to ensure that all students understand the process.

Have the students decode the ciphertext given in 11. Most students will have little difficulty in setting up the two equations, but some might meet with difficulty in solving for *a* and *b*. Turn this frustration into a discussion of the security of affine ciphers among people who do not know algebra. Use the situation to encourage the study of algebra.

Affine Ciphers. Hand out Student Sheet 5.3. Have each group compose and exchange ciphertexts with another group. Circulate among groups to ascertain that all students understand the process. Focus discussion on the security of affine ciphers to a pre-algebra population and the importance and usefulness of algebra in cryptanalysis.

Discussion Questions

1. If you have an equation with two unknowns, say *a* and *b,* why do you need two equations in order to solve for *a* and *b?*

2. What is the relationship between additive ciphers, multiplicative ciphers, and affine ciphers?

3. How secure would affine ciphers be among your friends? Among your family members?

Assessment Questions

1. Boris and Natasha have just discovered affine ciphers. Give an enciphering rule and the key of an affine cipher for them to use in mod 29. Include a cipher table. Compose a ciphertext that Natasha sends to Boris.

2. Suppose Dudley finds the ciphertext that Natasha sends to Boris. Explain the steps he would go through in order to decipher it. You may, but you do not need to, decipher the note.

3. Write a paragraph describing the security of affine ciphers in terms that a nonscientifically trained person could understand.

The War of Cryptographers

During the first world war (1914–1918), secret messages and spies played such an important role that the war is sometimes called "the war of cryptographers." It is estimated that hundreds of secret messages were passed each day throughout the war.

One of these coded messages is what brought the United States into the war. In 1914, British intelligence intercepted a coded telegram from German Foreign Minister Arthur Zimmerman to the Mexican Government. It consisted of a thousand numbered code groups. After much effort, a special group of British cryptanalysts deciphered the message and passed it on to the United States. The message promised Mexico money and the regions of Texas, Arizona, and New Mexico if they would, with Germany, declare war on the United States. The scheme prompted President Wilson to declare war.

Soon after, the United States organized a force of cryptanalysts under the direction of Herbert Yardley. Yardley and his staff were amazingly successful. In one year, they deciphered 813 Japanese telegrams that had been enciphered in 11 different systems. At first, they did their work in a secret room, nicknamed the American Black Chamber.

With the success of code breaking in World War I, everyone realized the importance of having more difficult ciphers and better ways to encode and decode information. By World War II, technology was bringing encoding machines, microfilm, and other inventions to the field of cryptography.

A Cryptic History

History is filled with examples of cryptography having an impact on events. Mary Queen of Scots sent enciphered letters to a friend revealing a plot to assassinate Queen Elizabeth I of England. When a letter was captured, and easily decoded, Mary was beheaded.

During the American Civil War, Union cryptanalysts claimed to have solved every secret message from the Confederate army. The Confederates, however, had to publish some captured Union messages in the newspaper as puzzles for the readers to help solve.

During World War II, a team of cryptanalysts, including world-famous William Friedman, decrypted Japanese messages made by a cipher machine the United States code named *Purple*. Deciphering the Japanese Purple Code greatly impacted the course of the war.

Do some research to find another example of how cryptography has influenced historical events. Write a short essay on your findings.

A Fine Cipher This Is

1. An affine cipher is of the form $C \equiv a \times P + b \bmod d$, where a and b are positive integers and a is relatively prime to d (that is, a and d have no factors in common). The ciphertext given below has been encoded with an affine cipher mod 26. Determine a and b. The plaintext has been given the following numerical equivalents.

	A	B	C	D	E	F	G	H	I	J	K	L	M
P	1	2	3	4	5	6	7	8	9	10	11	12	13

	N	O	P	Q	R	S	T	U	V	W	X	Y	Z
P	14	15	16	17	18	19	20	21	22	23	24	25	26

Decode the ciphertext and respond in plaintext.

S Z E J   D M L Q   S E G   M G Q N   J U   Q R K U N Q   J Z C G   R U J Q ?

2. What strategies are you using to decode the cipher text?

3. Complete the chart for the above affine cipher as best you can.

$(a, b) = $ _____

	A	B	C	D	E	F	G	H	I	J	K	L	M
C													

	N	O	P	Q	R	S	T	U	V	W	X	Y	Z
C													

4. How secure is this cipher?

A Fine Decipher System

1. As a group, read and discuss the following method to break affine ciphers. Continue the discussion until each member of the group understands the process.

   On student sheet 5.1, you were given the ciphertext:

   SZEJ DMLQ SEG MGQN JU QRKUNQ JZCG RUJQ?

   the plaintext values A = 1, B = 2, . . . , Z = 26, and the fact that an affine cipher of the form $C \equiv a \times P + b \bmod 26$ was used to create the ciphertext. You were to determine a and b and use those values in the equation to create a cipher table.

   One of your first steps was probably to check the frequencies of the letters in the ciphertext. You found that Q was the most frequently used letter (occurring 5 times) and J was the next most frequent (4 times). You probably hypothesized that Q stood for E and J for T.

   This is exactly what a cryptanalyst would do. As soon as she has a hypothesis about the most frequent letters, she uses her knowledge of algebra to determine the enciphering rule.

   For example, hypothesizing that E $\rightarrow$ Q, she substitutes E's numerical value (5) for P and Q's numerical value (17) for C in the rule for an affine cipher, resulting in

   $$17 \equiv a \times 5 + b \bmod 26 \text{ or } 17 \equiv 5a + b \bmod 26$$

   Next, hypothesizing that J stood for T, she substitutes their numerical values (10 and 20) for P and C, giving another equation,

   $$10 \equiv a \times 20 + b \bmod 26 \text{ or } 10 \equiv 20a + b \bmod 26$$

   She now has two equations in two unknowns. One way to solve for a and b is to graph both equations on the same pair of coordinate axes. The point where the two equations intersect gives the values for a and b that are common to both equations. These values of a and b will make both equations true.

   Describe any limitations on the values of a and b.

A Fine Decipher System

2. You have learned that $5 \times 3 + 16 \bmod 26 \equiv 15 + 16 \bmod 26$

$$\equiv 31 \bmod 26$$
$$\equiv 5 \bmod 26$$
$$\equiv 5 + 26 \bmod 26.$$

Similarly, $17 \bmod 26 \equiv 17 + 26 \bmod 26$, and therefore $17 \equiv 5a + b \bmod 26$ is equivalent to $17 + 26 \equiv 5a + b \bmod 26$.

Write two other statements equivalent to $17 \equiv 5a + b \bmod 26$.

3. You will graph these equations. The graph of the first equation will be all the pairs (a, b) for which $5a + b \equiv 17$. The second will be all the pairs of (a, b) for which $5a + b \equiv 17 + 26 \equiv 43$. The third plot will be all the pairs of (a, b) for which $5a + b \equiv$ ____. Imagine how the plots will look. Hypothesize how these plots will be related.

4. Compute at least three pairs of (a, b) for three of the equivalent equations.

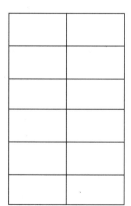

$17 \equiv 5a + b$ _____ $\equiv 5a + b$ _____ $\equiv 5a + b$

A Fine Decipher System

Graph these equations in the same color on the same coordinate axes. Write the equation on each plot.

a. Do the plots look as you hypothesized they would?

b. Describe any patterns you notice.

5. Now do the same for the other equation: $10 \equiv 20a + b \bmod 26$.

a. Write two other statements equivalent to $10 \equiv 20a + b \bmod 26$.

b. Hypothesize how the plots will look, and how they will be related.

c. Compute at least three pairs of (a, b) for three of the equivalent equations.

$10 \equiv 20a + b$ ___ $\equiv 20a + b$ ___ $\equiv 20a + b$

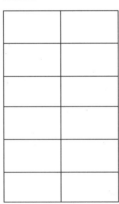
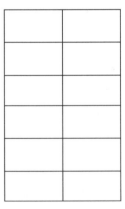

d. Using the same coordinate axes but a different color, graph these equations. Write the equation on each plot.

A Fine Decipher System

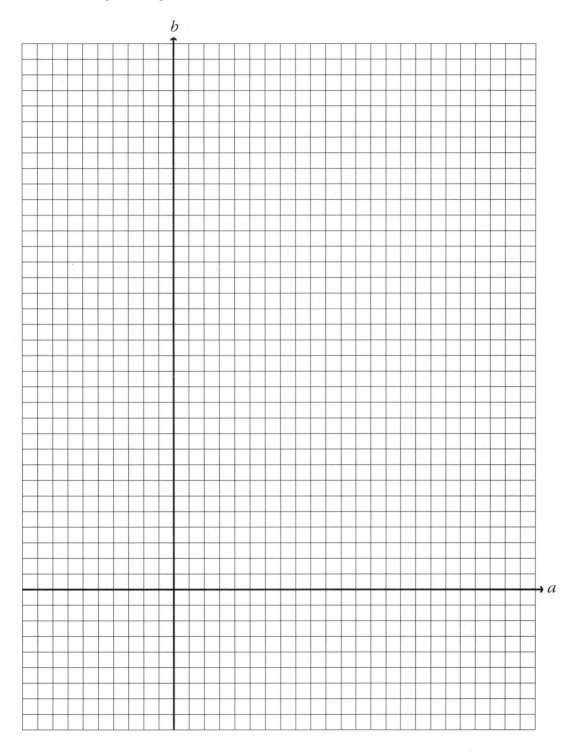

A Fine Decipher System

6. Do any of the plots intersect?

   a. If so, what is the value for (a, b) at one point of intersection?

   b. Could this be a possible solution to this problem? Explain your reasoning.

7. Select another point of intersection and decide if it is a possible solution. Continue this process until you discover a solution that satisfies the conditions on a and b.

8. Substitute the values for a and b in the general equation to find the enciphering rule.

   $C \equiv$ _____ $\times P +$ _____ mod 26

9. This enciphering rule was used to encode the ciphertext and it can be used to decode it. Use the enciphering rule to complete the cipher table.

(a, b) = _____

	A	B	C	D	E	F	G	H	I	J	K	L	M
C													

	N	O	P	Q	R	S	T	U	V	W	X	Y	Z
C													

10. The following ciphertext was encoded with the same rule. Use the cipher table to decode it. Then answer the question.

    ZUS OERY MRCAMQ OUN VVPC ETTCRQ

    KCXZQDG EDQ XUGGCHLQ? QVXLECR.

11. Decode the following ciphertext. It was encoded using an affine cipher mod 26. Give the enciphering rule, the cipher table, and the plaintext.

    MFWZ WOZ RZPBMTWV XE WOTR PTCOZM XS F

    RPFIZ XE XSZ WX WZS.

$$(a, b) = \_\_\_$$

	A	B	C	D	E	F	G	H	I	J	K	L	M
C													

	N	O	P	Q	R	S	T	U	V	W	X	Y	Z
C													

A Fine Decipher System

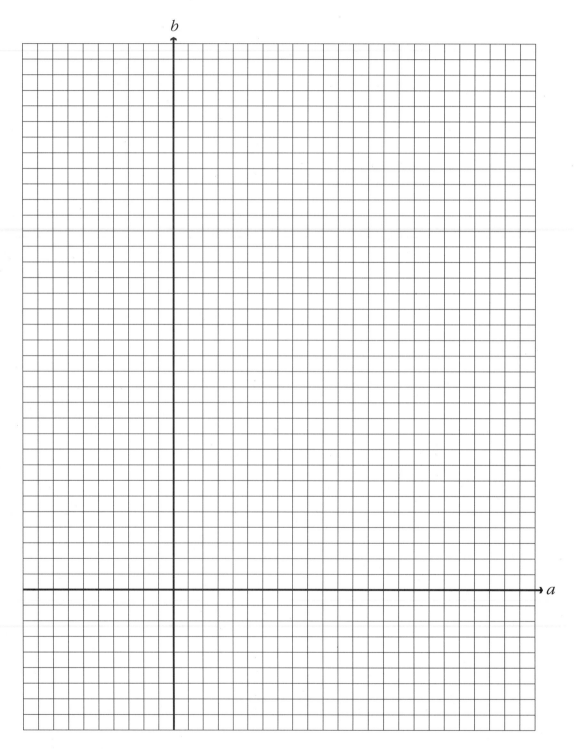

Affine Ciphers

1. Develop a new affine cipher. Record the rule below.

2. Complete the cipher table for your cipher rule.

$$(a, b) = \text{_____}$$

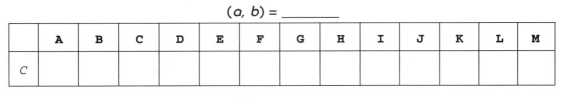

	A	B	C	D	E	F	G	H	I	J	K	L	M
C													

	N	O	P	Q	R	S	T	U	V	W	X	Y	Z
C													

3. As a group, develop a short message. Write the plaintext below.

4. Encode the plaintext with your unique affine cipher. Write the ciphertext below. Also write it on another piece of paper.

5. Exchange ciphertexts with another group. Decode the received ciphertext. Write the enciphering rule, the cipher table, and the plaintext below.

6. How secure is this cipher?

VIGENÈRE CIPHERS

Overview

Students discover that the Vigenère Cipher is no more than a combination of multiple additive ciphers. Vigenère Ciphers, like affine ciphers, are easy to encode but difficult to decode without the key. Students verify that once they determine the length of the keyword, they can then decode the ciphertext. Vigenère Ciphers, however, are not as well known to middle schoolers as the additive ciphers, and therefore, are more secure. Many middle schoolers will be enthusiastic about this cipher.

Time. One to two 45-minute periods.

Purpose. The Vigenère Cipher is the basis for the one-time pad, a cipher with a significant role in history and one still in use today. The Vigenère Cipher will interest many students, and its extension, the one-time pad, is an example of a cryptic system still in use by professional cryptographers today.

Materials. *For the teacher:*

◆ Transparencies of Student Sheets 6.1–6.2

For each student:

◆ Student Sheets 6.1–6.3

◆ Calculator

◆ Alberti Enciphering Machine (from Activity 1)

Getting Ready

1. Duplicate Student Sheets 6.1–6.3.
2. Locate calculators.
3. Prepare transparencies of Student Sheets 6.1–6.2.
4. Have students locate their enciphering machines.

Background Information

In this activity, students explore the Vigenère Cipher, which is a combination of multiple additive ciphers. Vigenère Ciphers, like affine ciphers, are easy to encode, but difficult to decode without the key. The Vigenère Cipher was invented in 1586 by a Frenchman named Blaise de Vigenère. It is a simple yet effective way to lessen the importance of letter frequency in decoding ciphertext.

In a Vigenère Cipher, the cryptographer needs two things: a Vigenère square and a keyword. A Vigenère square consists of all 26 additive ciphers, and is given on Student Sheet 6.1. Note that the Vigenère square is composed of all the ciphers you can make on your Alberti Enciphering Machine. The A cipher (the first row) is a shift of 0 (A → A) and the D cipher (the fourth row) is the Caesar Cipher.

You choose the keyword in this cipher. It can be any length, but each letter in the alphabet can only appear once. For example, *math* is a permissible keyword. *Mathematics* is not a possible keyword because the *m, a,* and *t* occur more than once. It can, however, be made into a keyword by omitting the repeated letters. *mathematics* → *matheics* becomes a permissible keyword.

Student Sheet 6.1 explains how to construct a Vigenère Cipher. While the Vigenère Cipher is difficult to decode if you do not know the keyword, it is easy to decode if you do know it. In addition, it becomes possible to decode the cipher if you know just the length of the keyword. Yes, this is true! Once you know the length of the keyword, the Vigenère Cipher can be decoded. Read through the rules and the example given on Student Sheet 6.1 before reading the material below on how to decode the Vigenère Cipher.

A Prussian colonel named Friedrich Wilhelm Kasiski invented the decoding method in 1863, nearly 300 years after the Vigenère Cipher was invented! So the Vigenère Cipher was truly secure for a long time, and is relatively secure today, at least to non-professionals.

The Kasiski method focuses on repeated sequences of three or more letters. It is based on the thinking that frequently used words such as *the* will be eventually enciphered by the same keyword letter in longer messages. Determining the length between repeated sequences can lead to determining the keyword length, and once you know the keyword length, you can determine the actual keyword. Once you know the length of the keyword, the deciphering consists of deciphering different additive shifts.

Follow the example of the Kasiski method on Student Sheet 6.2. It leads students through finding the length between repeated sequences, finding the factors of the lengths, and determining the length of the keyword. The example identifies the keyword as *math*.

Continuing with Student Sheet 6.2, to check the hypothesis that the keyword is *math,* decode the first few words of the ciphertext. For this example, we will represent letters in capitalized form so they will be easy to match with the ciphertext. The first column was encoded with the additive cipher that took A → M, called the *M cipher* or the *M row*. The first letter in the first column is F. Locate the ciphertext letter F in the M row and determine what column it is in, which gives you its plaintext equivalent. It is located in column T, so the first letter in the plaintext is T.

The next letter in the ciphertext is H, and it was encoded with cipher A, so it remains H. If you had forgotten this, then locate the position of H in the A row and discover that it is in column H, so H → H.

The third letter in the ciphertext is X and it was encoded with the T cipher. Locate X in the T row and find that it is in column E. So the third letter in the plaintext is E.

Continue in this fashion until you are certain the keyword is *math*. After the first few words make sense, and you are convinced of the keyword, change to a more efficient tactic.

```
                              T


                              T H




                              T H E


                              T H E C
                              A T I N
                              T H E H
                              A T
```

Now decipher the ciphertext column by column (or cipher by cipher). This is faster and produces less errors, even though it does not give you immediate feedback regarding the words in the plaintext. The first column was encoded with the additive cipher that took A → M, the M cipher or the M row. So every letter in the first column needs to be decoded using the M row. (This could be done with your Alberti Enciphering Machine.)

```
T
A
T
A
E
G
N
S
H
U
R
T
U
E
E
D
T
A
T
G
```

Now decode all the letters in the second column using the A cipher. This is easy, they all remain the same!

```
T  H
A  T
T  H
A  T
E  T
G  R
N  E
S  A
H  A
U  T
R  T
T  H
U  R
E  O
E  R
D  H
T  O
A  T
T  H
G
```

Then decode all the letters in the third column using the T cipher.

```
T  H  E
A  T  I
T  H  E
A  T  A
E  T  H
G  R  E
N  E  G
S  A  N
H  A  M
U  T  Y
R  T  L
T  H  E
U  R  T
E  O  B
E  R  V
D  H  O
T  O  N
A  T  C
T  H  E
G  G
```

And lastly, decode all the letters in the fourth column using the H cipher.

```
T  H  E  C
A  T  I  N
T  H  E  H
A  T  A  T
E  T  H  E
G  R  E  E
N  E  G  G
S  A  N  D
H  A  M  B
U  T  Y  E
R  T  L  E
T  H  E  T
U  R  T  L
E  O  B  S
E  R  V  E
D  H  O  R
T  O  N  H
A  T  C  H
T  H  E  E
G  G
```

On Student Sheet 6.3, students explore the Kasiski test further. The Technology Links "The Unbreakable Code" and "The Unbreakable Code—Broken" may be used at any time during this activity to further student interest.

Presenting the Activity

The Vigenère Cipher. Divide students into groups of four. This allows for partner work as well as many voices contributing to the discussion. Hand out Student Sheet 6.1 and have students locate their Alberti Enciphering Machines. Allow sufficient time for students to explore the Vigenère Cipher, including the Vigenère Square and the method for enciphering a plaintext. Students should have little difficulty understanding the Vigenère Square. As you circulate among the groups, make sure all students understand the use of the keyword and how to encipher a message. Use a transparency of Student Sheet 6.1 to go over the example of how to encode a Vigenère Cipher if you deem it necessary.

After students have composed and exchanged ciphertexts, observe groups deciphering the messages. If the ciphertext does not have repeated words that can be identified, students will not be able to decipher it. Also, if the plaintext does not have E and T occurring with the greatest frequency, students will still be able to decipher the note, but it will take more time to determine the keyword. If you judge a growing frustration level, have a class discussion focused on the security of the Vigenère Cipher, and then have groups exchange keywords.

As a class, discuss the security of the Vigenère Cipher and the difficulty to decode it without the key. Inform students that the code can be broken, if you know the trick. All they need to know is the length of the keyword. The next activity gives them an example.

The Kasiski Method. Hand out Student Sheet 6.2 and allow time for students to work through the example. As you circulate among groups, ascertain the level of understanding of the length between repeats and the common factors of the length. Do students understand why the hypothesized length of the keyword cannot be two? If necessary, work through the example using an overhead transparency of Student Sheet 6.2. Once the groups understand the process, have them decipher the message in question 2. The plaintexts of both these ciphertexts were constructed to ensure a predominance of *e*'s and *t*'s as well as obvious repeats. The plaintext students construct on Student Sheet 6.3 might not be so constructed, and the trial-and-error phase to find the keyword might take longer.

Using the Vigenère Cipher. Hand out Student Sheet 6.3. If you notice groups having difficulty with question 1, have a class discussion on the factors that make it difficult to decode a Vigenère Cipher.

For question 5, let students work on the new ciphertext for a while, then allow them to exchange keywords and continue their work.

Discussion Questions

1. How does a Vigenère square relate to the Alberti Enciphering Machine?

2. Why is the length of the keyword sufficient information to allow the deciphering of a Vigenère Cipher?

3. What could one do to maximize the security of a Vigenère Cipher?

Assessment Questions

1. Compose a 20-word plaintext that any student who has done this unit will be able to decode once it has been encoded with a Vigenère Cipher. Explain what makes it easily decodable.

2. Compose a plaintext that would be very difficult to decode even if you knew it had been encoded with a Vigenère Cipher. Explain what would make it so difficult to break.

3. Write a paragraph explaining why knowing the length of the keyword is enough to allow one to break a Vigenère Cipher.

4. Natasha learns about the Vigenère Ciphers. She still wants to keep a 29-symbol alphabet. Construct a Vigenère square for Natasha to use.

The Unbreakable Code

You have learned that you can break even difficult ciphers with knowledge of letter frequency and algebra, plus a little work. Is there a truly unbreakable code? Well, yes. One-time pads are codes that are used one time, for one message, and then destroyed. But these codes are time consuming to decipher, because the key is different for every message.

In 1975, two engineers at Stanford University created the very first unbreakable code that was easy to use. How unbreakable? They estimated that a computer program would have to run for millions of years in order to break it!

They called it the trap-door cipher because you need two keys. One key will encode the message, taking you through the door. But without the other key—a key completely different from the first—you cannot go "backward" through the door to decipher the message.

Three computer scientists at the Massachusetts Institute of Technology later improved the trap-door cipher using prime numbers. Their system is called the RSA cipher, and it is used in many businesses and government agencies to protect computer information.

In simple terms, here's how the RSA cipher works. First, pick two secret prime numbers; call them p and q. In actuality, p and q would be very large primes—more than a 100 digits each. Next, multiply p and q together, giving you n, the number that will be used as the modular base. Determine $(p-1)$ and $(q-1)$. Choose a number e, which will serve as the exponent, such that e has no common factors with either $p-1$ or $q-1$. Raise the numerical equivalent of each letter in the message (the plaintext) to e and write it as a mod n number. The letter equivalent of the mod n number becomes the letter in the ciphertext. Confusing? It should be. RSA ciphers need computers to encode the message.

Can you imagine a number that has 200 digits? How long do you think it would take you to write it? How long do you think it would take you to write it correctly? Today, it is estimated that it would take a computer more than your potential lifetime to factor it! So, this cipher is secure—for now!

Decoding the message, therefore, is a big problem. One needs to know the original two prime numbers to decode the message. It is not sufficient to know n; one needs to know the prime factors of n—p and q. And remember, we are

talking about numbers that are more than a hundred digits long. Super computers could try to break the code, but it would take them millions of years to find all the possible values for p and q if n is 200 digits long.

Now that you know a little about this new, unbreakable code, do you think it really is unbreakable?

In a public key cipher system, the key (e, n) is made public, but the two prime factors of n (p and q) are kept secret. The trick is to have p and q so large that even most computers could not determine them even if n is known. The significance of this cipher is that even if you knew the encoding key, it would take you too long to discover the primes in order to develop the decoding key.

The following is an example of a RSA cipher using two very small primes 3 (p) and 5 (q). When you multiply them together, you get 15, which is n, the mod. $p - 1 = 3 - 1 = 2$ and $q - 1 = 5 - 1 = 4$. Possible values for e are 3, 5, or 7, none of which have either 2 or 4 as a factor. Let $e = 7$, the value to which you raise the value of each letter in the plaintext.

Suppose the plaintext is COT = 3 15 20.

3^7 mod 15 = 12. Therefore, C $\rightarrow$ L.

15^7 mod 15 = 15. Therefore, O $\rightarrow$ O.

20^7 mod 15 = 5. Therefore, T $\rightarrow$ E.

The ciphertext is LOE.

Now, imagine this example where p and q are large. Once p and q are 2 or more digits long, it takes a computer to even encode the message. And decoding the ciphertext is a totally different problem that depends on being able to factor n. Imagine this example where p and q are 100 digits long, making n 200 digits long. In 1995, mathematicians made a breakthrough in using computers to approximate primes. While this did not immediately threaten the RSA cipher, cryptographers took no chances. They came back with even longer primes, and today the RSA cipher is still quite secure.

The Unbreakable Code—Broken

When three cryptographers from the Massachusetts Institute of Technology developed their RSA cipher, they believed they had created the perfect code—an unbreakable cipher. As a challenge, they printed this puzzle and offered $100 to anyone who could decipher it. (They estimated it would take about 40,000,000,000,000,000 years to crack!)

96,869,613,754,622,061,477,140,922,254,355,882,905,759,991,124,574,319,874, 695,120,930,816,298,225,145,708,356,931,476,622,883,989,628,013,391,990,551,829, 945,157,815,154

This message is encrypted in a public key system. This is how it works:

- You write a message to person A in plaintext. Let's say person A is another student.

- You encode the message using A's special encoding formula. The encoding formulas for all the students in your school would be published in a book, so you could send encoded messages to any other student. This is why it is called the public key system.

- A gets your message, but so does B who is spying and intercepts your message. B has the encoding formula, but that won't help. Only A has the decoding formula, so only A can decipher your message to read it.

The formulas involve a complex process of changing letters to numbers, then using very large prime numbers to create ciphertext, similar to the one above.

Was the $100 secret message unbreakable? It seemed to be, but it wasn't. More than 600 people, linked by computer, got together to sift through portions of possible solutions. After eight months, the combined effort was put into a super computer, which took 45 hours to figure out the two prime numbers that, when multiplied, led to the $100 message. Seconds later, it spit out the deciphered message:

"The magic words are squeamish ossifrage."

It was a nonsense message, but it made cryptographers realize that even the best unbreakable codes are, well, breakable.

The Vigenère Cipher

The Vigenère Cipher was invented in 1586 by a Frenchman named Blaise de Vigenère. It is a simple yet effective way to lessen the importance of letter frequency in decoding ciphertext. The A cipher is a shift of O.

In a Vigenère Cipher, the cryptographer needs two things:
- a Vigenère Square
- a keyword

Vigenère Square

		A	B	C	D	E	F	G	H	I	J	K	L	M	N	O	P	Q	R	S	T	U	V	W	X	Y	Z
		Plaintext
	a	a	b	c	d	e	f	g	h	i	j	k	l	m	n	o	p	q	r	s	t	u	v	w	x	y	z
	b	b	c	d	e	f	g	h	i	j	k	l	m	n	o	p	q	r	s	t	u	v	w	x	y	z	a
	c	c	d	e	f	g	h	i	j	k	l	m	n	o	p	q	r	s	t	u	v	w	x	y	z	a	b
	d	d	e	f	g	h	i	j	k	l	m	n	o	p	q	r	s	t	u	v	w	x	y	z	a	b	c
	e	e	f	g	h	i	j	k	l	m	n	o	p	q	r	s	t	u	v	w	x	y	z	a	b	c	d
	f	f	g	h	i	j	k	l	m	n	o	p	q	r	s	t	u	v	w	x	y	z	a	b	c	d	e
	g	g	h	i	j	k	l	m	n	o	p	q	r	s	t	u	v	w	x	y	z	a	b	c	d	e	f
	h	h	i	j	k	l	m	n	o	p	q	r	s	t	u	v	w	x	y	z	a	b	c	d	e	f	g
	i	i	j	k	l	m	n	o	p	q	r	s	t	u	v	w	x	y	z	a	b	c	d	e	f	g	h
	j	j	k	l	m	n	o	p	q	r	s	t	u	v	w	x	y	z	a	b	c	d	e	f	g	h	i
	k	k	l	m	n	o	p	q	r	s	t	u	v	w	x	y	z	a	b	c	d	e	f	g	h	i	j
	l	l	m	n	o	p	q	r	s	t	u	v	w	x	y	z	a	b	c	d	e	f	g	h	i	j	k
	m	m	n	o	p	q	r	s	t	u	v	w	x	y	z	a	b	c	d	e	f	g	h	i	j	k	l
	n	n	o	p	q	r	s	t	u	v	w	x	y	z	a	b	c	d	e	f	g	h	i	j	k	l	m
	o	o	p	q	r	s	t	u	v	w	x	y	z	a	b	c	d	e	f	g	h	i	j	k	l	m	n
	p	p	q	r	s	t	u	v	w	x	y	z	a	b	c	d	e	f	g	h	i	j	k	l	m	n	o
	q	q	r	s	t	u	v	w	x	y	z	a	b	c	d	e	f	g	h	i	j	k	l	m	n	o	p
	r	r	s	t	u	v	w	x	y	z	a	b	c	d	e	f	g	h	i	j	k	l	m	n	o	p	q
	s	s	t	u	v	w	x	y	z	a	b	c	d	e	f	g	h	i	j	k	l	m	n	o	p	q	r
	t	t	u	v	w	x	y	z	a	b	c	d	e	f	g	h	i	j	k	l	m	n	o	p	q	r	s
	u	u	v	w	x	y	z	a	b	c	d	e	f	g	h	i	j	k	l	m	n	o	p	q	r	s	t
	v	v	w	x	y	z	a	b	c	d	e	f	g	h	i	j	k	l	m	n	o	p	q	r	s	t	u
	w	w	x	y	z	a	b	c	d	e	f	g	h	i	j	k	l	m	n	o	p	q	r	s	t	u	v
	x	x	y	z	a	b	c	d	e	f	g	h	i	j	k	l	m	n	o	p	q	r	s	t	u	v	w
	y	y	z	a	b	c	d	e	f	g	h	i	j	k	l	m	n	o	p	q	r	s	t	u	v	w	x
	z	z	a	b	c	d	e	f	g	h	i	j	k	l	m	n	o	p	q	r	s	t	u	v	w	x	y

(Ciphers label appears on the left side of the square.)

© Washington MESA

The Vigenère Cipher

1. A Vigenère Square consists of all 26 additive ciphers. It is composed of all the ciphers you can make on your Alberti Enciphering Machine. The D cipher (the fourth row) is the Caesar Cipher. The A cipher is a shift of 0.

2. You choose the keyword. It can be any length, but each letter in the alphabet can only appear once. For example, *math* is a permissible keyword. *Mathematics* is not a possible keyword because the *m, a,* and *t* occur more than once. It can, however, be made into a keyword by omitting the repeated letters. *Mathematics* → *matheics* becomes a permissible keyword.

A Vigenère Cipher is constructed in the following way:

Rules	Example
Write the plaintext.	S E C R E T C O D E S A R E F U N
Decide on the keyword.	M A T H
Write the keyword repeatedly above the plaintext.	M A T H M A T H M A T H M A T H M S E C R E T C O D E S A R E F U N
The letter in the keyword above the plaintext determines which row in the Vigenère Square you will use to encipher just that letter. For example, the first letter in the plaintext is S and the letter in the keyword above it is M, so the row beginning with M is the cipher row for encoding S. Find the plaintext S and go down the column until you are in row M. The letter is E. Therefore, S → E in cipher M.	M A T H M A T H M A T H M A T H M S E C R E T C O D E S A R E F U N E
The second plaintext letter is E, the keyword letter above it is A, so the row beginning with A is the cipher row, and E remains E.	M A T H M A T H M A T H M A T H M S E C R E T C O D E S A R E F U N E E
Repeat the process until the ciphertext is completely encoded. Convince yourself that the plaintext is correctly enciphered.	M A T H M A T H M A T H M A T H M S E C R E T C O D E S A R E F U N E E V Y Q T V V P E L H D E Y B Z

NOTE: In a Vigenère Cipher, a letter in the ciphertext could stand for more than one letter in the plaintext!

The Vigenère Cipher

3. As a group, decide on a keyword and a short message. Write the plaintext below.

4. Write the plaintext below with no spaces. Write the keyword above the plaintext from beginning to end. Using the Vigenère Square, determine the ciphertext for each letter and write it below the plaintext.

5. Write the ciphertext on another piece of paper. Exchange ciphertexts with another group.

6. Decode the other group's ciphertext and write the plaintext below.

7. How secure is this code?

8. If you were not successful in decoding the ciphertext, obtain the keyword and decipher it now.

The Kasiski Method

1. As a group, read and discuss the following information on the Kasiski method to decode Vigenère Ciphers. Continue the discussion until each member of the group understands the process.

You might think the Vigenère Cipher is invincible, but cryptanalysts are clever people. A Prussian colonel named Friedrich Wilhelm Kasiski invented a method in 1863, nearly 300 years after the Vigenère Cipher was invented! So the Vigenère Cipher was truly secure for a long time, and is relatively secure today, at least to nonprofessionals. But you are about to become a professional cryptanalyst.

The Kasiski method focuses on repeated sequences of 3 or more letters. It is based on the thinking that frequently used words such as *the* will be eventually enciphered by the same keyword letter in longer messages. Determining the length between repeated sequences can lead to determining the keyword length, and once you know the keyword length, you can determine the actual keyword.

Kasiski Method	Example
Ciphertext	F H X J M T B U F H X O M T T A Q T A L S R X L Z E Z N E A G K T A F I G T R L D T E L F H X A G R M S Q O U Z Q R O L P H H Y F O G O M T V O F H X L S G
Search for repeated sequences.	F H X J M T B U F H X O M T T A Q T A L S R X L Z E Z N E A G K T A F I G T R L D T E L F H X A G R M S Q O U Z Q R O L P H H Y F O G O M T V O F H X L S G

The Kasiski Method

Kasiski Method	Example
Determine length between repeats.	F H X J M T B U F H X has 8 spaces between repeats F H X O M T T A Q T A L S R X L Z E Z N E A G K T A F I G T R L D T E L F H X has 36 spaces between repeats F H X A G R M S Q O U Z Q R O L P H H Y F O G O M T V F H X has 28 spaces between repeats
Factor each length into prime factors.	$8 = 2 \times 4 = 2 \times 2 \times 2$ $36 = 4 \times 9 = 2 \times 2 \times 3 \times 3$ $28 = 4 \times 7 = 2 \times 2 \times 7$
Determine the common factors.	2 is a common factor $2 \times 2 = 4$ is a common factor
The length of the keyword is most likely one of these common factors.	Discuss why this is true.
Each of these possibilities needs to be checked.	2 is a common factor, but 2 < 3 so it could not be the length of a keyword that would give repeats of length 3. Discuss this fact to make sure everyone understands.
Check out the common factor of 4.	The first step is to block the ciphertext into lengths of 4. This example uses 4 columns, but you could make 8 or 12 columns.

The Kasiski Method

Arrange the ciphertext into 4 columns.

```
F H X J
M T B U
F H X O
M T T A
Q T A L
S R X L
Z E Z N
E A G K
T A F I
G T R L
D T E L
F H X A
G R M S
Q O U Z
Q R O L
P H H Y
F O G O
M T V O
F H X L
S G
```

If the keyword were 4 letters long, then each column would represent that part of the ciphertext that had been encoded with the same cipher, and therefore, the frequency of occurrence of any letter should approximate the frequency of use in English (at least in a relatively large cipher). Although this ciphertext is really too short to do this, it will serve for demonstration.

Determine the most frequently occurring letter in each column.

F T X L

Assuming the most frequently used letter in each column is E, use the Vigenère Square to determine which cipher row it came from. For the first column, determine in which cipher row E → F. Cipher B takes E → F.

B

Which cipher takes E → T? Cipher P takes E → T.

P

Which cipher takes E → X? Cipher T takes E → X.

T

Which cipher takes E → L? Cipher H takes E → L.

H

The Kasiski Method

If E were the most frequently used letter in each cipher,
the BPTH would be the keyword, but BPTH is not a word,
so check the next most frequently used letter. The table on
Student Sheet 1.2 says T is the next most frequently used
letter. Check T next.

Cipher M takes T → F; cipher A takes T → T.   M A

Hypothesize the keyword is *math*.   M A T H

2. Verify the keyword is *math* and decode the ciphertext. Write the
   plaintext below.

3. Use your Vigenère Square to decode the following ciphertext.

NVWAWMFTAXOOSVGUBWLHQXOOMVWEMGZTAGJE

MXWAOMHHQVLEJXLHQCSRQXGBQIPCTEFGQHSN

PHWCAHWDGWWARYFEMWQKQCOODHSNPIFSGVWR

QTWAFIVSQUMEZGWSUXZEXTK

Using the Vigenère Cipher

1. Discuss with your group the factors that affect the security of the Vigenère Cipher. List them, and explain how each affects the security. Be prepared to present one of your factors to the class.

2. As a group, compose a message and write the plaintext below.

3. Determine a keyword. Write it below.

4. Encipher the plaintext. Write the ciphertext below and on another piece of paper.

5. Exchange ciphertexts with another group. Decode the received ciphertext and write the plaintext below.

6. If you could not determine the keyword, ask for a hint and continue.

FAMILY
ACTIVITY

WORMS AND
ONE-TIME PADS

Overview

Students review with their families the Caesar Cipher, letter frequencies, and additive ciphers. Very long keywords—equal in length to the plaintext—are introduced by having the families decode a ciphertext encoded using a line from the Interest Link as the keyword! The Vernam Cipher is a Vigenère Cipher with one very important extension. The keyword in a Vernam Cipher is a *worm*—a sequence of randomly selected letters, removing all influence of letter frequency. The Vernam Cipher is commonly known as the *one-time pad*. It has a significant history and is still in use today.

Time. Two to three evenings.

Purpose. The student's family learns about a cryptosystem that has a significant use in the history of our country and is still in use today. They learn of the extensive use of mathematics in cryptology.

Materials. *For each student:*

◆ Presenting the Activity Sheet
◆ Completed Student Sheet 1.2, 6.1, and 6.2 (for reference)

For each family:

◆ Family Activity Sheets 1–3
◆ 2 copies of Family Activity Sheet 4
◆ Interest Link "Steganography" (from page 112)
◆ Alberti Enciphering Machine (from Activity 1)
◆ History Link "One-Time Pads" (from page 111)
◆ Calculators
◆ Two dice, each of a different color

Getting Ready

1. Copy Presenting the Activity and Family Activity Sheet 1–3, 2 copies of 4.

2. Copy the Interest Link "Steganography" and the History Link "One-Time Pads."

3. Locate dice and calculators.

Background Information

In this family activity, students review with their families the Caesar Cipher, letter frequencies, and additive ciphers. Very long keywords—equal in length to the plaintext—are introduced by having families decode a ciphertext encoded using a line from the Interest Link as the keyword! The Vernam Cipher, commonly known as the one-time pad, is a Vigenère Cipher with one very important extension. The keyword in a Vernam Cipher is a *worm*—a sequence of randomly selected letters, removing all influence of letter frequency. The Vernam Cipher has a significant history, and it is still in use today.

On Family Activity Sheet 1, the family group is introduced to the Caesar Cipher in a manner similar to what students did on Student Sheet 1.2. After a discussion to ensure that all family members understand the Caesar Ciphers, the family divides into two groups. Each group composes and exchanges ciphertexts, and then decodes the received ciphertext.

Family Activity 2 introduces the family group to the Vigenère Cipher. The student shares the Vigenère square and the Kasiski test with the family. There is a ciphertext that has repeats for the group to decipher.

Family Activity 3 introduces very long keywords, which when employed with a Vigenère Cipher will significantly increase the difficulty of decoding a ciphertext. The groups are given a ciphertext that has no repeats. After exploring it, they are told that the keyword—the very long keyword—is actually a line from the Interest Link. With this knowledge, they can decode the message. At this point they should read the Interest Link "Steganography."

Family Activity 4 introduces the family group to keyword worms and provides a method for generating one. A worm that is as long as the message itself, removes all influence of letter frequency. It is theoretically unbreakable. If one, however, knows something about the content of the message, one might, with considerable persistence, decode it. The History Link "One-Time Pads" goes along well with this activity sheet.

Presenting the Activity

Explain to your family that together you will be investigating *cryptosystems* (methods of changing letters in and out of coded form), some of which are still in use today. Explain that you will be exploring the cryptosystems from two perspectives. One perspective is security: How difficult is it to decode a ciphertext if you do not know the key, if you don't know how it was enciphered? Another way to look at cryptosystems is how easy they are to use when you know the key. These two factors both come into play in the real world of spies, security communications, and cryptology. Make sure everyone in your family group understands the terminology.

The Caesar Cipher. Hand out Family Activity Sheet 1 and discuss the Caesar Cipher. Allow every member in your family group an opportunity to share in the decoding of the ciphertext. The message concerns the frequency of use of letters in the English language. After the message has been decoded, share the letter frequencies from Student Sheet 1.2. If it has not yet been discussed, bring up how the knowledge of the more frequently used letters aids in *cryptanalysis* (the process of translating a cryptogram when the code is unknown).

Explain that the Caesar Cipher is one of 26 different additive ciphers. Give an example of a different additive cipher.

The Vigenère Cipher. Explain that a Vigenère Cipher is a combination of different additive ciphers; different parts of the plaintext are encoded with different additive ciphers. Discuss that this is done to remove the influence of letter frequency. Hand out Family Activity Sheet 2 and explore with your family group the Vigenère Square. Share your Alberti Enciphering Machine, and point out the correspondence between the two.

Share your work on the Vigenère Cipher from Student Sheet 6.1, as well as your work on how to determine the length of the keyword from Student Sheet 6.2. It would probably be good to work through the entire example on Student Sheet 6.2 to ensure all family members understand the process. When your group is ready, decipher the message given at the bottom of the page. It does have repeats, so you will be able to decode it. Refer to Student Sheet 6.2 at any time you need to.

Family Activity 3 introduces material that is new to you. However, this is just an extension of the keyword associated with the Vigenère Cipher. In the examples you have had so far, the keyword was a real word, and it was probably relatively short. If the keyword is very long, however, the chance of repeats becomes small, and determining the length of the keyword becomes very difficult. In the extreme case, when the keyword is a string of words as long as the plaintext, the chance of repeats and therefore, the determination of the keyword becomes nearly impossible. Family Activity 3 introduces this idea.

Very Long Keywords. Try to decode the ciphertext before identifying the keyword. You probably won't be able to do so (even professional cryptanalysts would find it difficult). The text tells you where to locate the very long keyword. Identify it, and then decode the message.

The ultimate in very long keywords is called a *worm*. It is a string of randomly selected letters. The random selection of the letters removes all traces of letter frequency. A Vigenère Cipher created with a worm is known as a *one-time pad*. It is a very secure cipher that is still in use today. It was invented in 1917 by an American engineer named Gilbert S. Vernam. At some point, read the History Link on the Vernam Cipher, which has come to be known as the one-time pad.

The Vernam Cipher. Hand out 2 copies of Family Activity Sheet 4 and discuss the one-time pad and its relationship to the Vigenère Cipher. Point out that the only difference you will be introducing is the construction of the worm. Discuss that this is a major difference in terms of cryptanalysis. The use of the worm makes this cipher almost impossible to decode even for professional cryptographers.

Explain that you will eventually break into two groups; each group will generate·a short plaintext and a worm. When the ciphertexts have been completed, they will be exchanged and you will attempt to decipher them. Conclude the activity with a discussion of the security of this cryptosystem and its use throughout history, including its use today. And if you really want to decipher the message, be persistent or beg for the worm.

One-Time Pads

In 1953, a 13-year-old newspaper boy dropped one of his nickels. To his surprise, when he picked it up, he found it had split apart and a tiny piece of microfilm fell out. He gave the microfilm to police, who gave it to the FBI, who enlarged it to find it contained a message in Soviet code. Cryptanalysts tried desperately to decipher it, but they could not. The code was not broken until Reino Hayhanen, a soviet spy, turned himself in at an American embassy. He revealed that the message was intended for him, and that he had the key.

The message was part of a sophisticated cryptosystem Soviet spies were using. In part, it involved a cipher method called a *one-time pad,* a booklet of random numbers. When you receive an enciphered message, you use a prespecified page in the booklet to decode the message. Then you throw the page away. The key is used just "one time." Anyone trying to break the code would probably never be able to decipher the message because the key uses random numbers. And even if the person did get the key, it would only work on one message. The one-time pad was truly an unbreakable code.

The one-time pad was used often during World War II. Hayhanen's superior was the high-level Soviet officer and spy, Rudolph Ivanovich Abel. After Abel was arrested, a tiny one-time pad was found in a hollow block of wood thrown in his trash.

During the war, U.S. and British agents put one-time pads on tiny pieces of film or silk, so the numbers could only be read with a magnifying glass. By the 1960s, entire pads were the size of a postage stamp. Some were printed on paper and microfilmed so they would fit inside such things as hollow bolts.

One-time pads are effective as unbreakable codes, but they require massive amounts of time to create and use. Even today, these ciphers are used by spies and government for top-secret communication.

Steganography

When people in government, in the military, or in businesses want to communicate in code, they may send each other enciphered messages directly—by computer or radio for example. If the message is intercepted, the hope is that the intruder will not be able to break the code before the message is outdated.

But what if you did not want anyone knowing that you were sending or receiving messages? Even if the messages are encoded, you still want their existence to be a secret. *Steganography* is the art of hiding a secret message.

One example of steganography is invisible ink. Lemon juice and onion juice make good invisible inks. Apply heat and the messages reappear! George Washington used invisible inks in the American War of Independence to convey information to his agents. During the world wars, chemicals were used as invisible inks to write messages between the lines of newspapers or letters.

Two ancient Greeks reportedly used stenography to conspire a revolt. They shaved the head of a slave and tattooed a message on it. When his hair grew back, they sent him to conspirators, who shaved his head to read the message.

With the invention of microfilm, long messages could be printed on pieces of film as small as the period at the end of this sentence. Microfilm messages have been hidden in hollowed out bolts, in a hollow tooth, and under postage stamps. In World War II, Allies sent messages into Nazi territory by hiding them in a hole in a key.

The Caesar Cipher

1. Julius Caesar invented one of the earliest known secret codes. The following message was encoded using the Caesar Cipher. Decode it and write it below.

   H   LV   WKH   PRVW   IUHTXHQWOB   XVHG

   OHWWHU   LQ   HQJOLVK,   DQG   W   LV   QHAW.

2. Discuss the decoding process to make sure everyone in your family understands it.

3. Discuss the Caesar Cipher encoding rule to make sure everyone in your family understands it.

4. Divide into 2 groups. Each group should compose a message and write the plaintext here.

   - - - - - - - - - - - - - Tear here after you complete question 5. - - - - - - - - - - - -

5. Using the Caesar Cipher, encode the plaintext and write the ciphertext here.

6. Tear the paper between questions 4 and 5. Exchange ciphertexts with the other group. Decode the received ciphertext and write the plaintext below.

7. Discuss the procedures you used to encode and decode the messages. Outline the critical points of the procedures you used.

The Vigenère Cipher

1. Discuss the Vigenère Cipher with your family group. Refer to Student Sheet 6.1. Include in the discussion the following information:
   a. Vigenère Square (share Student Sheet 6.1)
   b. Keyword
   c. Letter frequency (share Student Sheet 1.2)
   d. Kasiski method (share Student Sheet 6.2)

Vigenère Square

	Plaintext																									
	A	B	C	D	E	F	G	H	I	J	K	L	M	N	O	P	Q	R	S	T	U	V	W	X	Y	Z
	a	b	c	d	e	f	g	h	i	j	k	l	m	n	o	p	q	r	s	t	u	v	w	x	y	z
	b	c	d	e	f	g	h	i	j	k	l	m	n	o	p	q	r	s	t	u	v	w	x	y	z	a
	c	d	e	f	g	h	i	j	k	l	m	n	o	p	q	r	s	t	u	v	w	x	y	z	a	b
	d	e	f	g	h	i	j	k	l	m	n	o	p	q	r	s	t	u	v	w	x	y	z	a	b	c
	e	f	g	h	i	j	k	l	m	n	o	p	q	r	s	t	u	v	w	x	y	z	a	b	c	d
	f	g	h	i	j	k	l	m	n	o	p	q	r	s	t	u	v	w	x	y	z	a	b	c	d	e
	g	h	i	j	k	l	m	n	o	p	q	r	s	t	u	v	w	x	y	z	a	b	c	d	e	f
	h	i	j	k	l	m	n	o	p	q	r	s	t	u	v	w	x	y	z	a	b	c	d	e	f	g
	i	j	k	l	m	n	o	p	q	r	s	t	u	v	w	x	y	z	a	b	c	d	e	f	g	h
	j	k	l	m	n	o	p	q	r	s	t	u	v	w	x	y	z	a	b	c	d	e	f	g	h	i
	k	l	m	n	o	p	q	r	s	t	u	v	w	x	y	z	a	b	c	d	e	f	g	h	i	j
Ciphers	l	m	n	o	p	q	r	s	t	u	v	w	x	y	z	a	b	c	d	e	f	g	h	i	j	k
	m	n	o	p	q	r	s	t	u	v	w	x	y	z	a	b	c	d	e	f	g	h	i	j	k	l
	n	o	p	q	r	s	t	u	v	w	x	y	z	a	b	c	d	e	f	g	h	i	j	k	l	m
	o	p	q	r	s	t	u	v	w	x	y	z	a	b	c	d	e	f	g	h	i	j	k	l	m	n
	p	q	r	s	t	u	v	w	x	y	z	a	b	c	d	e	f	g	h	i	j	k	l	m	n	o
	q	r	s	t	u	v	w	x	y	z	a	b	c	d	e	f	g	h	i	j	k	l	m	n	o	p
	r	s	t	u	v	w	x	y	z	a	b	c	d	e	f	g	h	i	j	k	l	m	n	o	p	q
	s	t	u	v	w	x	y	z	a	b	c	d	e	f	g	h	i	j	k	l	m	n	o	p	q	r
	t	u	v	w	x	y	z	a	b	c	d	e	f	g	h	i	j	k	l	m	n	o	p	q	r	s
	u	v	w	x	y	z	a	b	c	d	e	f	g	h	i	j	k	l	m	n	o	p	q	r	s	t
	v	w	x	y	z	a	b	c	d	e	f	g	h	i	j	k	l	m	n	o	p	q	r	s	t	u
	w	x	y	z	a	b	c	d	e	f	g	h	i	j	k	l	m	n	o	p	q	r	s	t	u	v
	x	y	z	a	b	c	d	e	f	g	h	i	j	k	l	m	n	o	p	q	r	s	t	u	v	w
	y	z	a	b	c	d	e	f	g	h	i	j	k	l	m	n	o	p	q	r	s	t	u	v	w	x
	z	a	b	c	d	e	f	g	h	i	j	k	l	m	n	o	p	q	r	s	t	u	v	w	x	y

The Vigenère Cipher

2. As a group, decode the following ciphertext. Write the plaintext below.

   (Hint: The keyword is a common noun. Remember, no repeats allowed.)

   V H R Y G I E A H P G C V S F G R H V C F W V W F C L R Q E V H L N

   C A W B U B K S F W G N L H V C F T B G Y A S B P C V I Z H Q V H R

   N C A W B U B K S R Y C P G E H Y V E E W F C N A L L G T L Q G P E

   Y H R V E E V G P L R Q E V H

Very Long Keywords

You have probably discovered that there are 2 or 3 things you could do to make the Vigenère Cipher quite difficult to decode. For instance, you could composed a ciphertext without repeated sequences; you could use very few *e*'s or *t*'s in the message; your plaintext could have a high frequency of rarely used letters, such as *v, k, j, x, q,* and *z;* and you could use a very long keyword.

While all these factors contribute to the difficulty of decoding the ciphertext, it is the last one that can lead to a truly secure cipher. The longer the keyword, the less chance of repeated sequences and a smaller chance to have *e*'s and *t*'s dominate each cipher. The extension of a very long keyword is the concept of a keyword that is as long as the ciphertext itself. This idea has been used by professional cryptographers.

One way to create a keyword that is as long as the plaintext (and therefore, also as long as the ciphertext) is to identify (by code, of course) a passage in a novel, or an encyclopedia, or any identifiable prose. For instance, the following ciphertext was encoded with the keyword that begins with the first letter of the third sentence of the text in the Interest Link "Steganography."

1. Write the third sentence of the Interest Link text above the ciphertext. Decode it, and write the plaintext below the ciphertext.

Keyword from Link

Ciphertext

   X B T P J I I P J P K U V C V R R M D E Z H S G G B R R M B R E V T Z A P S G M H Y

Plaintext

2. Discuss the significance of the message.

3. Discuss how secure this type of cipher is.

4. Discuss how you would exchange keywords if you were trying to exchange secret messages with a friend.

The Vernam Cipher

While using a passage from a text as a keyword results in a fairly secure ciphertext, a professional cryptanalyst would be able to eventually decode it based on letter frequency. In 1917, Gilbert S. Vernam, an American engineer, invented a cryptosystem that removes all influence of letter frequency. The Vernam Cipher, which has become known as the one-time pad, is an extension of the Vigenère Cipher in which the keyword is a worm. It consists of a sequence of letters chosen at random. The use of a worm results in a theoretically secure cipher. Knowing the cipher for one letter does not give you any information to help you find the cipher for any other letter.

The one-time pad has been an important and widely used cryptosystem and is still used today. It was used by the English to secretly transmit the decoded German messages during the latter part of World War II, and it has been rumored that the "hot line" between the White House and the Kremlin during the Cold War relied on the one-time pad. Even today, with multiple systems being used, the one-time-pad remains one of the systems in use.

Worms

You could roll a 26-sided die, each side having a letter of the alphabet on it, to create a worm, or you could use a computer to generate a worm. In this module, we will use two different-colored dice and this table to generate a worm.

The Vernam Cipher

Worm Code	Die color 1					
Die color 2	**1**	**2**	**3**	**4**	**5**	**6**
1	A	B	C	D	E	*
2	F	G	H	I	J	*
3	K	L	M	N	O	*
4	P	Q	R	S	T	*
5	U	V	W	X	Y	*
6	*	*	*	*	*	Z

*Ignore all rolls with a 6, unless it is a double 6.

1. Generate a worm that is as long as your name. Write it below.

2. Break into 2 groups.

3. Each group compose a short message and write the plaintext below.
   Worm

   Plaintext

   Ciphertext

4. Generate a worm and write it above the plaintext.

5. Create the ciphertext and write it below the plaintext.

The Vernam Cipher

6. Write the ciphertext below.

7. Exchange ciphertexts and attempt to decode.

8. Discuss how secure this cipher is.

9. If you did not break the code, get the worm.

10. Discuss how someone who uses this cipher would transmit the keyword.

11. The one-time pad is not often used even though it is a secure code. Discuss why this is so.

COMPLETED
STUDENT
SHEETS

Letter Frequencies

1. Not all letters are used with the same frequency in any natural language. In English, *e* is the most frequently used letter in novels and newspapers, occurring with a frequency of nearly 13 percent. The following table gives the letters by their relative frequencies of use in English.

Frequency of Use in English

Letters	Approximate Frequency of Each Letter
E	13%
T	9%
A, O	8%
I, N	7%
S, H, R	6%
D, L	4%
C, U	3%
M, W, F, G, Y, P	2%
B, V, K, J	1%
X, Q, Z	<1%

2. Cryptanalysis is the process of figuring out secret codes and ciphers. Discuss how knowing the frequency of use of the letters aids in cryptanalysis.
If you know which letters are more likely to be used, you could substitute those into the ciphertext as your first tries.

The Caesar Cipher

1. Caesar invented one of the earliest known secret codes. A secret code is also called a cipher. The following message was encoded (written in code) using the Caesar Cipher. Decode it and write it below.

Z K D W   L V   W K H   P R V W   I U H T X H Q W O B   X V H G

O H W W H U   L Q   H Q J O L V K ?

What is the most frequently used letter in English?

2. Describe the decoding rule for the above message.
Each letter is replaced with the third letter before it in the alphabet. For example, D is replaced with A.

3. Describe the encoding rule called the Caesar Cipher.
Each letter is replaced with the third letter after it in the alphabet. For example, A is replaced with D.

4. As a group, compose a message and write it below. Using the Caesar Cipher, encode your message and write it below. Also write the encoded message on another piece of paper.
Answers will vary.

5. Exchange coded messages with another group. Write the coded message you received below. Decode it and write the decoded message below the encoded one.
Answers will vary.

6. Discuss with your group the procedures you used to encode and decode the messages. Outline the critical points of the procedures you used.
Critical points could include letter frequency, testing small words, looking for patterns, and so on.

Numerical Enciphering

1. Alberti made his enciphering machine using letters. It is common in *cryptography* (the study and practice of making messages secret) to assign the following numerical values to each letter in the alphabet: A = 1, B = 2, C = 3, . . . , Z = 26. Write the numerical value for each letter below and also on your enciphering machine.

   A = 1, B = 2, C = 3, D = 4, E = 5, F = 6, G = 7, H = 8, I = 9, J = 10, K = 11, L = 12, M = 13, N = 14, O = 15, P = 16, Q = 17, R = 18, S = 19, T = 20, U = 21, V = 22, W = 23, X = 24, Y = 25, Z = 26

2. What is the numerical value of Y?
   Y = 25

3. What is the Caesar Cipher equivalent of Y?
   The letter B

4. What is the numerical value for the Caesar Cipher equivalent of Y?
   B = 2

5. In Activity 1, you learned one way to write a rule for a Caesar Cipher: P + 3 → C. Write a numerical rule for the Caesar Cipher that takes into account what happens to Y.
   There are many possible rules. One might be
   P + 3 → C where P = 1, 2, . . . , 23 and P + 3 − 26 → C for P = 24, 25, 26

6. Write a numerical rule with regard to Y for an additive shift of 12.
   P + 12 → C

7. Give an example of a common use of an additive shift 12. It need not be related to a code.
   Time on a 12-hour clock (12 noon, 1 o'clock, and so on); Navy time; (4 bells, 8 bells, 12 bells, 4 bells, . . .) months in a year

8. Do you know a mathematical convention for writing a numerical shift such as the ones above? Discuss with your group. Make an educated guess, and write it down. Then read the Interest Link "Modular Arithmetic."
   C ≡ P + 3 mod 26

Me Caesar—You Decode

1. The Caesar Cipher is a shift. Each letter of the alphabet is replaced with the third letter after it. A → D, B → E, and so on. One way to write the rule could be:

   P + 3 → C where P is any letter in the plain alphabet and C is its coded form.

   Note that X + 3 → A, Y + 3 → B, and Z + 3 → C. The Caesar Cipher is an additive shift of +3. It could also be described as an additive shift of ⁻23.

2. As a group, decide what shift you would have used, had you been Caesar. Write the rule for encoding a message with your shift.
   Answers will vary.

3. As a group, develop a short (10-word, 75-letter maximum) message. Write the message below.
   Answers will vary.

4. Encode the message with your modified Caesar shift. Write the encoded message below. Also write it on another piece of paper.
   Answers will vary.

5. Exchange encoded messages with another group. Decode the message you received. Write both the encoded and decoded forms of the message below.
   Answers will vary.

6. What is the rule for decoding the other group's message?
   Answers will vary.

7. What is the rule that was used to encode the message?
   Answers will vary.

8. What is the relationship between the encoding and decoding rules?
   The encoding and decoding rules are the inverse of each other. The decoding rule undoes what the encoding rule does.

9. To say a code is *secure* means the coded message is very difficult to figure out for anyone who does not have the key. How secure is the other group's code?
   This code is not very secure. It can be broken with trial-and-error methods.

Mod Arithmetic

1. A mathematical rule for the numerical equivalent of the Caesar Cipher (shift 3) could be written as follows:

C = P + 3 mod 26, where P is the numerical value for any letter in the plaintext and C is its equivalent in the ciphertext. The symbol ≡ means congruence. For example, we know that 2 ≠ 28, but 2 ≡ 28 mod 26. In mod 26, 2 and 28 have equivalent values.

The interpretation of this rule, C = P + 3 mod 26, is exactly what you have been doing.

Modular Addition	C = P + 3 mod 26
Take any number P	for example P = 25
add 3 to it	25 + 3 = 28
subtract 26 (mod value) until the difference is between 1 and 26	28 − 26 = 2
C = the difference	C = 2

You have probably heard many names for modular arithmetic—clock arithmetic, remainder arithmetic, modular arithmetic, and modulus arithmetic. They are all perfectly valid labels. In this module, we are going to use the term modular arithmetic, or sometimes mod arithmetic for short.

2. How many different values are there for C in mod 26? List them.
There are 26 values: 1, 2, . . ., 26.

3. How many different values are there for C in mod 7? List them.
There are 7 values: 1, 2, . . ., 7.

Mod Arithmetic

4. Determine C in each of the following number sentences.

   a. C ≡ 6 + 3 mod 7   b. C ≡ 2 + 3 mod 7
      C ≡ 2   C ≡ 5
   c. C ≡ 6 + 1 mod 7   d. C ≡ 6 + 6 mod 7
      C ≡ 7   C ≡ 5

5. Find five different pairs (a, b) that satisfy the number sentence a + b mod 7 = 4.
Answers will vary. Some possibilities include: 4 ≡ 0 + 4 mod 7; 4 ≡ 1 + 3 mod 7; 4 ≡ 2 + 2 mod 7; and 4 ≡ 10 + 8 mod 7.

6. Make an addition table mod 7. Write it in the grid below.

Addition Mod 7

+	1	2	3	4	5	6	7	8	9	10
1	2	3	4	5	6	7	1	2	3	4
2	3	4	5	6	7	1	2	3	4	5
3	4	5	6	7	1	2	3	4	5	6
4	5	6	7	1	2	3	4	5	6	7
5	6	7	1	2	3	4	5	6	7	1
6	7	1	2	3	4	5	6	7	1	2
7	1	2	3	4	5	6	7	1	2	3
8	2	3	4	5	6	7	1	2	3	4
9	3	4	5	6	7	1	2	3	4	5
10	4	5	6	7	1	2	3	4	5	6

7. As a group, analyze the addition mod 7 table. Record your observations. *Observations could include the following: repeated rows, repeated columns, diagonals (/) are the same number, and each column and row has every pos-*

Mod Arithmetic

8. Are any of the rows and columns in this table repeats? If you crossed out any repetitive rows or columns, would you lose any information? Explain.
There are repeated rows, and you lose no information because 8 = 1, 9 = 2, and so on. These are repeats.

9. In regular addition, 0 is the additive identity. Explain what that means. If you do not know the term additive identity, research it.
When the additive identity is added to any number, that number does not change. Or a more formal definition: The additive identity (i) is that number such that any number n when added to i remains n, that is, n + i = n.

10. Are there any 0s in your addition mod 7 table? Is there a number that acts as an additive identity? If so, what is it? Give an example to support your response.
There are no 0s, but 7 acts as 0 in regular addition. That is, n + 7 = n for all n.

11. Complete the addition mod 7 table.

Addition Mod 7

+	1	2	3	4	5	6	7
1	2	3	4	5	6	7	1
2	3	4	5	6	7	1	2
3	4	5	6	7	1	2	3
4	5	6	7	1	2	3	4
5	6	7	1	2	3	4	5
6	7	1	2	3	4	5	6
7	1	2	3	4	5	6	7

Mod Arithmetic

12. Is the table in question 11 a complete mod 7 addition table? Explain.
Yes, it is complete. There are only 7 digits in mod 7, so a 7 × 7 table is all that is needed. Any other columns or rows would be repeats of what is already here.

13. What is an additive inverse? Research it, if necessary.
If a number is added to its additive inverse, the sum is the additive identity. Or a more formal definition: The additive inverse a is that number such that n + a = i (the additive identity).

14. Discuss with your group what the additive inverse for 3 mod 7 would be. Record your conclusion and explain your thinking.
Explanations might vary, but the additive inverse of 3 mod 7 is 4.

15. List the additive inverse for each number.
The additive inverse for 1 is 6, for 2 is 5, for 3 is 4, for 4 is 3, for 5 is 2, for 6 is 1, and for 7 is 7.

16. Subtraction is the inverse of addition: 2 − 4 mod 7 ≡ ? and 4 + ? mod 7 ≡ 2. Discuss with your group how you would use the addition mod 7 table to do subtraction mod 7. Explain, giving an example to illustrate.
2 − 4 mod 7 = 5. Procedures and other examples will vary.

17. What is 3 − 6 mod 7? Explain your procedure and give another example to illustrate it.
Possible answers: 3 − 6 mod 7 = 4. I know 4 + 6 mod 7 = 3. The inverse of addition is subtraction, so I locate the 3 in the body of the table that is in the 6 column, and I note that it is in row 4. 3 − 6 mod 7 = 4.

Multiplication Mod 7

1. Using what you know about the formula for modular addition, what do you think 6 × 4 mod 7 is? Explain, and give another example to illustrate.
   Take 6 × 4 = 24. Divide by the mod (÷ 7) = 3 with a remainder of 3. The remainder is the answer. Therefore, 6 × 4 mod 7 = 3. Examples will vary.

2. Determine C in each of the following number sentences.

   a. C ≡ 5 × 3 mod 7
   (5 × 3) ÷ 7 = 2 rem 1
   C ≡ 1

   b. C ≡ 2 × 3 mod 7
   (2 × 3) ÷ 7 = 0 rem 6
   C ≡ 6

   c. C ≡ 6 × 4 mod 7
   (6 × 4) ÷ 7 = 3 rem 3
   C ≡ 3

   d. C ≡ 6 × 6 mod 7
   (6 × 6) ÷ 7 = 5 rem 1
   C ≡ 1

3. List 5 different pairs (a, b) that satisfy the number sentence a × b mod 7 ≡ 4. *Answers will vary. Possible pairs include (2, 2), (4, 1), (1, 4), (5, 5), and (6, 3).*

4. Make a multiplication table mod 7. Write it in the grid below.

Multiplication Mod 7

×	1	2	3	4	5	6	7
1	1	2	3	4	5	6	7
2	2	4	6	1	3	5	7
3	3	6	2	5	1	4	7
4	4	1	5	2	6	3	7
5	5	3	1	6	4	2	7
6	6	5	4	3	2	1	7
7	7	7	7	7	7	7	7

Multiplication Mod 7

5. As a group, analyze the multiplication mod 7 table. Record your observations.
   Responses could include: Each row and column have each digit and the diagonals have different numbers, and the pattern of multiples is there (for instance in the row showing multiplication by 2, it goes 2, 4, 6, 1, 3, 5, 7).

6. In regular arithmetic, what is the multiplicative identity (the identity element with respect to multiplication)? Explain.
   The multiplicative identity is that number i such that n × i = i for all n. In regular multiplication, i = 1.

7. What is the multiplicative identity mod 7? Give an example to illustrate.
   The multiplicative identity in mod 7 is also 1.

8. What is a multiplicative inverse? Research it, if necessary.
   When a number is multiplied by its inverse, the product is 1. Or a more formal definition: The multiplicative inverse of n is that number m such that n × m = 1.)

9. List the multiplicative inverse for each number in mod 7.
   The multiplicative inverse for 1 in mod 7 is 1, for 2 is 4, for 3 is 5, for 4 is 2, for 5 is 3, and for 6 is 6. A multiplicative inverse for 7 does not exist.

10. Division is the inverse of multiplication: 2 ÷ 4 mod 7? and 4 × ? mod 7 = 2. Discuss with your group how you would use the addition mod 7 table to do subtraction mod 7. Explain, giving an example to illustrate.
    2 ÷ 4 mod 7 ⌐ 4. Procedures will vary.

11. What is 5 ÷ 4 mod 7? Explain your procedure, and give another example to illustrate it.
    5 ÷ 4 mod 7 ≡ 3. I know 4 × 3 mod 7 = 5. The inverse of multiplication is division, so I locate the 5 in the body of the table that is in the 4 column, and I note that it is in row 3. Therefore, 5 ÷ 4 mod 7 ≡ 3.

Mod Arithmetic Revisited

1. What is the commutative property of addition? Explain, and give an example to illustrate.
   The commutative property of addition states that for any numbers a and b, a + b = b + a. For example 1 + 2 = 2 + 1 = 3.

2. Is addition mod 7 commutative? Explain, and give an example to illustrate.
   Yes, addition mod 7 is commutative. It does not matter in which order you add the numbers. 5 + 3 mod 7 ≡ 3 + 5 mod 7 ≡ 1.

3. What is the associative property of addition? Explain, and give an example to illustrate.
   The associative property of addition states that for any numbers a, b, and c, a + (b + c) = (a + b) + c. The order in which you do the respective additions does not matter.

4. Is addition mod 7 associative? Explain, and give an example to illustrate.
   Yes, addition mod 7 is associative. 5 + (3 + 4) mod 7 ≡ 5 + 0 mod 7 ≡ 5 and (5 + 3) + 4 mod 7 ≡ 1 + 4 mod 7 ≡ 5.

5. Is addition in any mod arithmetic commutative and associative? Explain, and give examples to illustrate.
   Yes. Examples should involve other modular bases, such as 3, 5, 11, and 13.

Mod Arithmetic Revisited

6. What is the commutative property of multiplication? Explain, and give an example to illustrate.
   The commutative property of multiplication states that for any numbers a and b, b × a = a × b.

7. Is multiplication mod 7 commutative? Explain, and give an example to illustrate.
   Yes, multiplication mod 7 is commutative. It does not matter in which order you multiply the numbers. 5 × 3 mod 7 ≡ 3 × 5 mod 7 ≡ 1.

8. What is the associative property of multiplication? Explain, and give an example to illustrate.
   The associative property of multiplication states that for any numbers a, b, and c, a × (b × c) = (a × b) × c. The order in which you do the respective operations does not matter.

9. Is multiplication mod 7 associative? Explain, and give an example to illustrate.
   Yes, multiplication mod 7 is associative. 5 × (3 × 4) mod 7 ≡ 5 × 5 mod 7 ≡ 4 and (5 × 3) × 4 mod 7 ≡ 1 × 4 mod 7 ≡ 4.

10. Is multiplication in any mod arithmetic commutative and associative? Explain, and give examples to illustrate.
    Yes. Examples should involve other modular bases, such as 3, 5, 11, and 13.

Mod 4, 6, 8: What Do Spies Appreciate?

1. What is special about the number 7? Discuss as a group, and explain your conclusions.

   It is prime.

2. How does the number 7 differ from 4, 6, or 8? Discuss as a group, and explain your conclusions.

   Students may note that 7 is not even and it is not divisible by other numbers except 1 and itself. Students may realize that this constitutes a prime number.

3. Make a multiplication table mod 4, 6, or 8. You choose which of these mods you want to investigate. Write it in the grid below.

Multiplication Mod _6_

×	1	2	3	4	5	6
1	1	2	3	4	5	6
2	2	4	6	2	4	6
3	3	6	3	6	3	6
4	4	2	6	4	2	6
5	5	4	3	2	1	6
6	6	6	6	6	6	6

4. Analyze the multiplication mod ___ table. Compare it to the multiplication mod 7 table. Record your observations.

   Since 4, 6, and 8 are not relatively prime to 26, all these multiplication tables will consist of many repeats. Each row and column will not have each digit.

Mod 4, 6, 8: What Do Spies Appreciate?

5. What is the multiplicative identity mod ___? Explain.

   The multiplicative identity will be 1 in each of the above mods.

6. Does every number have a multiplicative inverse? Explain.

   No. There are some numbers p for which no n exists such that $n \times p = 1$. There are rows and columns that have no 1s.

7. What is 2 ÷ 2 mod 4 (or 6, or 8)?

   $2 \div 2 \bmod 4 \equiv 1, 3, 5,$ or 7. Regardless of the specific numbers, it will not be unique, there will be multiple values.

8. Can you be sure what 2 ÷ 2 mod 4 (or 6, or 8) is?

   No, it is not unique.

9. Which mod do you prefer? Explain.

   Answers will vary.

10. Which mod would a spy prefer? Explain.

    Spies would prefer mod prime systems. Actually, they prefer systems in which the mod is relatively prime to the multiplicative shift values. This will be addressed in the next activity.

Mod Multiplication on a Calculator

1. One efficient method to perform modular multiplication on a calculator is shown here:

Problem	Step	Calculation
$11 \times 25 \bmod 26$	1. Multiply numbers.	$11 \times 25 = 275$
	2. Divide by mod value.	$275 \div 26 = 10.57692308$
	3. Subtract integral part.	$10.57692308 - 10 = 0.57692308$
	4. Multiply by mod value.	$0.57692308 \times 26 = 15$

Therefore, $11 \times 25 \bmod 26 = 15$.

2. Discuss with your group why this works. Explain.
   You have subtracted out the multiples of 26, and in mod multiplication, it is the remainder that becomes the mod value.

3. Practice modular multiplication on the calculator.

   a. $7 \times 23 \bmod 26 \equiv$
   $7 \times 23 \div 26 = 6.19230769$
   $- 6 = .19230769$
   $\times 26 = 5$

   b. $5 \times 17 \bmod 26 \equiv$
   $5 \times 17 \div 26 = 3.269230769$
   $- 3 = .269230769$
   $\times 26 = 7$

   c. $11 \times 25 \bmod 23 \equiv$
   $11 \times 25 \div 23 = 11.95652714$
   $- 11 = .95652714$
   $\times 23 = 22$

   d. $11 \times 25 \bmod 29 \equiv$
   $11 \times 25 \div 29 = 9.472758621$
   $- 11 = .472758621$
   $\times 29 = 14$

4. Compose and solve 2 modular multiplication problems on the calculator.
   Answers will vary.

5. What is $6 \times 26 \bmod 26$?
   26

The Alberti Machine Revisited

Each ciphertext has been encoded using the Alberti Enciphering Machine. Decode and respond in plaintext.

1. H S L E X Z Z O O Z P D E S P L W M P C E T X L N S T Y P
   F D P ?
   The plaintext is: What mod does the Alberti Machine use?
   The key is: $C \equiv P + 11 \bmod 26$.
   The response is: The Alberti Machine uses mod 26.

2. O V D T H U F K P M M L Y L U A H K K P A P C L Z O P M M A Z
   H Y L W V Z Z P I S L V U H U H S I L Y A P T H J O P U L ?
   The plaintext is: How many different additive shifts are possible on an Alberti Machine?
   The key is: $C \equiv P + 7 \bmod 26$.
   The response is: The Alberti Machine has 26 possible shifts. However, shift 26 is never used.

3. V Q H S D S G D M T L D Q H B Q T K D E N Q S G H R
   Z C C H S H U D R G H E S .
   The plaintext is: Write the numeric rule for this additive shift.
   The key is: $C \equiv P + 25 \bmod 26$.

4. H I W G V M F I E Q Y P X M T P M G E X M Z I W L M J X E R H
   A V M X I E V Y P I .
   The plaintext is: Describe a multiplicative shift and write a rule.
   The key is: $C \equiv P + 4 \bmod 26$.
   The response is: $C \equiv k \times P \bmod 26$.

5. J V G U L B H E T E B H C Q R G R E Z V A R U B J G B Z B Q
   Z H Y G V C Y V P N G V B A B A G U R P N Y P H Y N G B E . B H G Y -
   V A R G U R F G R C F V A C Y N V A G R K G .
   The plaintext is: With your group determine how to do mod multiplication on the calculator. Outline the steps in plaintext.
   The key is: $C \equiv P + 13 \bmod 26$.
   The responses will vary.

Multiplicative Shifts

1. A multiplicative shift is of the form $C \equiv k \times P$ mod 26, where k is a positive integer. The ciphertext given below has been encoded with a multiplicative shift mod 26. The following numerical values were assigned to the plaintext. Hint: $k < 10$.

	A	B	C	D	E	F	G	H	I	J	K	L	M
P	1	2	3	4	5	6	7	8	9	10	11	12	13

	N	O	P	Q	R	S	T	U	V	W	X	Y	Z
P	14	15	16	17	18	19	20	21	22	23	24	25	26

Decode the ciphertext and respond in plaintext.
QXCH AE G AP HXAE MKJHAVJAICHANO EXARH?

The plaintext is: What is k in this multiplicative shift?
The key is: $C \equiv 3 \times P$ mod 26.
The response is: The k is 3.

2. Complete the cipher table for the above multiplicative shift.

$$k = 3$$

	A	B	C	D	E	F	G	H	I	J	K	L	M
P	1	2	3	4	5	6	7	8	9	10	11	12	13
C	3	6	9	12	15	18	21	24	1	4	7	10	13

	N	O	P	Q	R	S	T	U	V	W	X	Y	Z
P	14	15	16	17	18	19	20	21	22	23	24	25	26
C	16	19	22	25	2	5	8	11	14	17	20	23	26

Multiplicative Shifts

3. Discuss any patterns you observe in the cipher table. Report your conclusions.
The values of C occur in multiples of 3.

4. Some multiplicative shifts are better than others. As a group, explore the following multiplicative shifts:
a. $C \equiv 4 \times P$ mod 26

$$k = 4$$

	A	B	C	D	E	F	G	H	I	J	K	L	M
C	4	8	12	16	20	24	2	6	10	14	18	22	0

	N	O	P	Q	R	S	T	U	V	W	X	Y	Z
C	4	8	12	16	20	24	2	6	10	14	18	22	0

b. $C \equiv 5 \times P$ mod 26

$$k = 5$$

	A	B	C	D	E	F	G	H	I	J	K	L	M
C	5	10	15	20	25	4	9	14	19	24	3	8	13

	N	O	P	Q	R	S	T	U	V	W	X	Y	Z
C	18	23	2	7	12	17	22	1	6	11	16	21	0

Multiplicative Shifts

c. $C \equiv 6 \times P \bmod 26$ $k = 6$

A	B	C	D	E	F	G	H	I	J	K	L	M
5	10	15	20	25	4	9	14	19	24	3	8	13

N	O	P	Q	R	S	T	U	V	W	X	Y	Z
18	23	2	7	12	17	22	1	6	11	16	21	0

d. $C \equiv 7 \times P \bmod 26$ $k = 7$

A	B	C	D	E	F	G	H	I	J	K	L	M
7	14	21	2	9	16	23	4	11	18	25	6	13

N	O	P	Q	R	S	T	U	V	W	X	Y	Z
20	1	8	15	22	3	10	17	24	5	12	19	0

5. Which of the above multiplicative shifts would you prefer to use? Explain.
Students should recognize the benefit of using multiplicative shifts where $k = 5$ or 7 because they produce unique values for C.

More About Multiplicative Shifts

1. JIS MKXO MIR DDHU MWBLJUTBUGKLJUHC AJUNL GUTJCPA KPC LJCPC?
The plaintext is: How many mod xxvi multiplicative shift ciphers are there?
The key is: C ≡ 11 × P mod 26.
The response is: There are 26 multiplicative shift ciphers in mod 26.

2. JIS MKXO MIR DDHU MWBLJUTBUGKLJUHC AJUNLA YUHC IXC LI IXC LPKXABKLUIXA? XKMC LJCM.
The plaintext is: How many mod xxvi multiplicative shifts give one to one transla-tions? Name them.
The key is: C ≡ 11 × P mod 26.
The response is: There are 12 multiplicative shifts that yield a one-to-one correspondence: 1, 3, 5, 7, 9, 11, 15, 17, 19, 21, 23, and 25.

3. EDGJ BA SAQ TAJKUI GNAQJ JDI MAB LLXK MQFJKHFKUGJKXI CDKPJC JDGJ VICQFJ KT ATI JA ATI JVGTCFGJKATC?
The plaintext is: What do you notice about the mod xxvi multiplicative shifts that result in one to one translations?
The key is: C ≡ 7 × P mod 26.
The response is: They are relatively prime to 26, that is they have no factor in common with 26.

4. DAEMGTSUKHDIV JGNFIC EAQFB SAQ DGXI JA MGYI KT AVBIV JA BIUABI GTS MAB LLXK MQFJKHFKUGJKXI CDKPJ UKHDIV?
The plaintext is: How many cipher tables would you have to make in order to decode any mod xxvi multiplicative shift cipher?
The key is: C ⌈ 7 ¥ P mod 26.
The response is: You would have to make 11 cipher tables. A shift of 1 does not require decoding!

5. VYU WQEIDQ SDQ MITPORTOESPOBQ WVOJP EORVQDW?
(Hint: An A in ciphertext would be a K in plaintext: K Æ A.)
The plaintext is: How secure are multiplicative shift ciphers?
The key is: C ⌈ 19 ¥ P mod 26.
The response is: Multiplicative shifts are more secure than additive shifts, but they are not very secure at all. They can be broken by trial and error.

COMPLETED STUDENT SHEET 4.1

Prime Time

1. Take one tile. Convince yourself that you can make only one rectangle using one tile. Sketch the rectangle below.
   Students should sketch a square one unit by one unit here.
   What are the dimensions of the rectangle?
   one unit by one unit.

2. Take two tiles. Determine how many unique rectangles you can make with the two tiles. Sketch them below.
   Student may assume the two orientations are unique rectangles.

3. If a rectangle can be made to fit exactly on top of another rectangle, the two rectangles are said to be *congruent*. They are considered to be the same, they are not unique. With this note, examine your conclusions in 2. How many unique rectangles can you make with two square tiles?
   Just 1 unique rectangle.

4. What is a factor? What are the factors of 2? What is the relationship between the factors of 2 and the dimensions of the rectangles made with two tiles?
   A factor of a number divides the number. The factors are 1 and 2. These are the dimensions of the rectangle 1 unit by 2 units.

5. Continuing in this manner, determine how many unique rectangles you can make with three tiles, four tiles, and so on. For each number of tiles, record in the table on the next page the number of unique rectangles, the dimensions of each rectangle, and the factors of each number.

COMPLETED STUDENT SHEET 4.1 (cont'd)

Prime Time

Number of Tiles	Number of Unique Rectangles	Dimensions of Each Rectangle	Factors	Prime
1	1	1 × 1	1	
2	1	1 × 2	1, 2	P
3	1	1 × 3	1, 3	P
4	2	1 × 4, 2 × 2	1, 2, 4	C
5	1	1 × 5	1, 5	P
6	2	1 × 6, 2 × 3	1, 2, 3, 6	C
7	1	1 × 7	1, 7	P
8	2	1 × 8, 2 × 4	1, 2, 4, 8	C
9	2	1 × 9, 3 × 3	1, 3, 9	C
10	2	1 × 10, 2 × 5	1, 2, 5, 10	C
11	1	1 × 11	1, 11	P
12	3	1 × 12, 2 × 6, 3 × 4	1, 2, 3, 4, 6, 12	C
13	1	1 × 13	1, 13	P
14	2	1 × 14, 2 × 7	1, 2, 7, 14	C
15	2	1 × 15, 3 × 5	1, 3, 5, 15	C
16	3	1 × 16, 2 × 8, 4 × 4,	1, 2, 4, 8, 16	C
17	1	1 × 17	1, 17	P
18	3	1 × 18, 2 × 9, 3 × 6	1, 2, 3, 6, 9, 18	C
19	1	1 × 19	1, 19	P
20	3	1 × 20, 2 × 10, 4 × 5	1, 2, 4, 5, 10, 20	C

Primes Unlimited

1. Complete the tables on this page and the next page.

Num.	Num. of Rect.	Dimensions or Factors	Prime	Num.	Num. of Rect.	Dimensions or Factors	Prime
21	2	1, 3, 7, 21		41	1	1, 41	P
22	2	1, 2, 11, 22		42	4	1, 2, 3, 6, 7, 14, 21, 42	
23	1	1, 23	P	43	1	1, 43	P
24	4	1, 2, 3, 4, 6, 8, 12, 24		44	3	1, 2, 4, 11, 22, 44	
25	2	1, 5, 25		45	3	1, 3, 5, 9, 15, 45	
26	2	1, 2, 13, 26		46	2	1, 2, 23, 46	
27	2	1, 3, 9, 27		47	1	1, 47	P
28	3	1, 2, 4, 7, 14, 28		48	5	1, 2, 3, 4, 6, 8, 12, 16, 24, 48	
29	1	1, 29	P	49	2	1, 7, 49	
30	4	1, 2, 3, 5, 6, 10, 15, 30		50	3	1, 2, 5, 10, 25, 50	
31	1	1, 31	P	51	2	1, 3, 17, 51	
32	3	1, 2, 4, 8, 16, 32		52	3	1, 2, 4, 13, 26, 52	
33	2	1, 3, 11, 33		53	1	1, 53	P
34	2	1, 2, 17, 34		54	4	1, 2, 3, 6, 9, 18, 27, 54	
35	2	1, 5, 7, 35		55	2	1, 5, 11, 55	
36	4	1, 2, 3, 4, 9, 12, 18, 36		56	4	1, 2, 4, 7, 8, 14, 28, 56	
37	1	1, 37	P	57	2	1, 3, 19, 57	
38	2	1, 2, 19, 38		58	2	1, 2, 29, 58	
39	2	1, 3, 13, 39		59	1	1, 59	P
40	4	1, 2, 4, 5, 8, 10, 20, 40		60	6	1, 2, 3, 4, 5, 6, 10, 12, 15, 20, 30, 60	

Prime Time

6. As a group, examine the table. What is the relationship between number of rectangles, dimensions of rectangles, and factors? Explain.
The factors are in one-to-one correspondence to the dimensions of the rectangles.

7. What is a *prime number?* If you are not certain, research it. As a group, write a definition of a prime number.
A prime number is a number that has two and only two factors—1 and itself.

8. What is a *composite number?* If you are not certain, research it. As a group, write a definition of a composite number.
A composite number has more than two factors.

9. Label the last column in your table "Prime." Determine which numbers are prime and which numbers are composite. Put a *P* in the Prime column for each prime number and a *C* for each composite.

10. Is 1 prime? Explain.
Students may come up with arguments for why 1 is prime (it creates 1 unique rectangle, and it is only divisible by 1 and itself). However, in mathematics, 1 is defined as a special number, not a prime. It is the only number with only one factor and the only rectangle is a square.

2. How many prime numbers are there between 1 and 100? List them.
   There are 25 primes between 1 and 100. They are 2, 3, 5, 7, 11, 13, 17, 19, 23, 29, 31, 37, 41, 43, 47, 53, 59, 61, 67, 71, 73, 79, 83, 89, and 97.

3. Is 101 prime? Explain.
   Yes, it is a prime because 2, 3, 5, 7, and 11 are not factors of it.

4. Do you know any quick checks to determine if a number is prime? List at least three quick checks. If you do not readily come up with three checks, research it.
   The responses could include the following:
   - *If the number is even, then it is a multiple of 2.*
   - *If the digits of a number sum to a multiple of 3, then it is a multiple of 3.*
   - *If the number ends in 0 or 5, then it is a multiple of 5.*

5. Use your quick checks to determine if any numbers between 102 and 110 are prime. List any primes you find.
   The primes are 103, 107, and 109.

Primes Unlimited

Num.	Num. of Rect.	Dimensions or Factors	Prime	Num.	Num. of Rect.	Dimensions or Factors	Prime
61	1	1, 61	p	81	3	1, 3, 9, 27, 81	
62	2	1, 2, 31, 62		82	2	1, 2, 41, 82	
63	3	1, 3, 7, 9, 21, 63		83	1	1, 83	p
64	4	1, 2, 4, 8, 16, 32, 64		84	6	1, 2, 3, 4, 6, 7, 12, 14, 21, 28, 42, 84	
65	2	1, 5, 13, 65		85	2	1, 5, 17, 85	
66	4	1, 2, 3, 6, 11, 22, 33, 66		86	2	1, 2, 43, 86	
67	1	1, 67	p	87	2	1, 3, 29, 87	
68	3	1, 2, 4, 17, 34, 68		88	4	1, 2, 4, 8, 11, 22, 44, 88	
69	2	1, 3, 23, 69		89	1	1, 89	p
70	4	1, 2, 5, 7, 10, 14, 35, 70		90	6	1, 2, 3, 5, 6, 9, 10, 15, 18, 30, 45, 90	
71	1	1, 71	p	91	2	1, 7, 13, 91	
72	6	1, 2, 3, 4, 6, 8, 9, 12, 18, 24, 36, 72		92	3	1, 2, 4, 23, 46, 92	
73	1	1, 73	p	93	2	1, 3, 31, 93	
74	2	1, 2, 37, 74		94	2	1, 2, 47, 94	
75	3	1, 3, 5, 15, 25, 75		95	2	1, 5, 19, 95	
76	3	1, 2, 4, 19, 38, 76		96	6	1, 2, 3, 4, 6, 8, 12, 16, 24, 32, 48, 96	
77	2	1, 7, 11, 77		97	1	1, 97	p
78	4	1, 2, 3, 6, 13, 26, 39, 78		98	3	1, 2, 7, 14, 49, 98	
79	1	1, 79	p	99	3	1, 3, 9, 11, 33, 99	
80	5	1, 2, 4, 5, 8, 10, 16, 20, 40, 80		100	5	1, 2, 4, 5, 10, 20, 25, 50, 100	

A Fine Cipher This Is

1. An affine cipher is of the form $C \equiv a \times P + b \bmod d$, where a and b are positive integers and a is relatively prime to d (that is, a and d have no factors in common). The ciphertext given below has been encoded with an affine cipher mod 26. Determine a and b. The plaintext has been given the following numerical equivalents.

A	B	C	D	E	F	G	H	I	J	K	L	M
P	1	2	3	4	5	6	7	8	9	10	11	12	13

N	O	P	Q	R	S	T	U	V	W	X	Y	Z
P	14	15	16	17	18	19	20	21	22	23	24	25	26

Decode the ciphertext and respond in plaintext.

SZEJ DMLQ SEG MGQN JU QRKUNQ JZCG RUJQ?

The plaintext is: What rule was used to encode this note?

The key is: $C \equiv 3 \times P + 2 \bmod 26$.

Students may not be able to decode this ciphertext until they receive the rule.

2. What strategies are you using to decode the cipher text? *Answers will vary.*

3. Complete the chart for the above affine cipher.

$$(a, b) = (3, 2)$$

A	B	C	D	E	F	G	H	I	J	K	L	M
C					Q								

N	O	P	Q	R	S	T	U	V	W	X	Y	Z
C							J						

4. How secure is this cipher? *Answers will vary.*

Prime Sieve

1. Follow the directions below to determine all the prime numbers between 1 and 103.

   a. Circle all the primes in the first row.

   b. Draw a line through the first column (except for the 2) and through the entire third and fifth columns.

   c. Draw a line through the second column (except for the 3).

   d. Draw a diagonal line down and to the left (/) between 5 in the top row (but not actually through the 5 itself) and the first 5 in the left column. Draw parallel diagonal lines between pairs of 5s in the side columns.

   e. Draw a diagonal line down and to the right (\) between the first 7 in the left column and the first 7 in the right column. Do this again for the second 7s.

   f. Circle any number that does not have a line through it.

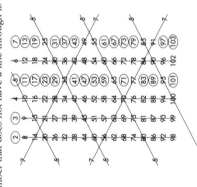

2. Explain why you are left with just the primes.

   You are left with just the primes because you have crossed out all the multiples of primes less than 10—2, 3, 5, and 7. And 10 is the square root of 100.

The response is: There are 12 different multiplicative shifts (one for each number relatively prime to 26) and 26 different additive shifts. Therefore, there are 26 × 12 = 312 possible affine ciphers. Nearly one for each day of the year!

11. Decode the following ciphertext. It was encoded using an affine cipher mod 26. Give the enciphering rule, the cipher table, and the plaintext.

MFWZ WOZ RZPBMTWV XE WOTR PTCOZM XS F
RPFIZ XE XSZ WX WZS.

(a, b) = (5, 1)

A	B	C	D	E	F	G	H	I	J	K	L	M
F	K	P	U	Z	E	J	O	T	Y	D	I	N

N	O	P	Q	R	S	T	U	V	W	X	Y	Z
S	X	C	H	M	R	W	B	G	L	Q	V	A

COMPLETED STUDENT SHEET 5.2

A Fine Decipher System

1. Describe any limitations on the values of *a* and *b*.
   Answers will vary. Possible answer: a and b are positive integers.

2. Write two other statements equivalent to $17 \equiv 5a + b \bmod 26$.
   Possible answers: $69 \lfloor 5a + b \bmod 26$ and $95 \lfloor 5a + b \bmod 26$.

3. *Answers will vary.*

4.b. Describe any patterns you notice.
   Students should notice that the lines are parallel.

5–7. *Answers will vary.*

8. Substitute the values for *a* and *b* in the general equation to find the enciphering rule.
   $C \equiv 3 \times P + 2 \bmod 26$

9. This enciphering rule was used to encode the ciphertext and it can be used to decode it. Use the enciphering rule to complete the cipher table.

(a, b) = (3, 2)

A	B	C	D	E	F	G	H	I	J	K	L	M
C	E	H	K	N	Q	T	W	Z	C	F	I	O

N	O	P	Q	R	S	T	U	V	W	X	Y	Z
R	U	X	A	D	G	J	M	P	S	V	Y	B

10. The following ciphertext was encoded with the same rule. Use the cipher table to decode it. Then answer the question.

ZUS OERY MRCAMQ OUN VVPC ETTCRQ
KCXZQDG EDQ XUGGCHLQ? QVXLECR.

Plaintext is: *HOW MANY UNIQUE MOD XXVI AFFINE*
CIPHERS ARE POSSIBLE? EXPLAIN.

The Vigenère Cipher

2. As a group, decode the following ciphertext. Write the plaintext below. (Hint: The Keyword is a common noun. Remember, no repeats allowed.)

VHRYGIEAHPGCVSFGRHVCFWVWFCLRQEVHLN
CAWBUBKSFWGNLHVCFTBGYASBPCVIZHQVHR
NCAWBUBKSRYCPGEHYVEEWFCNALLGTLQGPE
YHRVEEVGPLRQEVH

The keyword is: candy
The plaintext is: The Vigenère cipher used with a lengthy keyword is still used today sometimes the keyword is even greater than ninety nine letters in length.

---

1. Write the third sentence of the Interest Link text above the ciphertext. Decode it, and write the plaintext below the ciphertext.

Keyword from Link BUTWHATIFYOUDIDNOTWANTANYO
NEKNOWINGTHATYOU

Ciphertext   XBTPJIIPJPKUVCVRRMDEZHSGGB
RRMBREVTZAPSGMHY

Plaintext   WHATCIPHERWASUSEDTHEMOSTIN
ENCODINGTHISNOTE

2. Discuss the significance of the message.
The answers will vary, but the significance is related to the fact that the frequency of use in English dictates the frequency of ciphers used. The influence of letter frequency is lessened, but it is not totally removed.

3 and 4. Answers will vary.

The Kasiski Method

2. Verify the keyword is math and decode the ciphertext. Write the plaintext below.
The plaintext is: The cat in the bat ate the green eggs and bam but Yertle the turtle observed Horton hatch the egg.

3. Use your Vigenère Square to decode the following ciphertext.
NVWAWMFTAXOOSVGUBWLHQXOOMVWEMGZTAG-
JEMXWAOMHHQVLEJXLHQCSRQXGBQIPCTEFGQHSNP
HWCAHWDGWWARYFEMWQKQCOODHSNPIFSGVWRQT-
WAFIVSQUMEZGWSUXZEXTK.
The keyword is: mesa.
The plaintext is: Break into two groups the two are each to create a ciphertext they are to be exchanged and decoded use a fun easy keyword and ensure repeated sequences it helps.

The Caesar Cipher

1. Julius Caesar invented one of the earliest known secret codes. The following message was encoded using the Caesar Cipher. Decode it and write it below.
HLV WKH PRVW IUHTXHQWOB XVHG OHWWHU
LQ HQJOLVK, DQG W LV QHAW.
The plaintext is: e is the most frequently used letter in English, and t is next.
The key is: C $\equiv$ P + 3 mod 26.
2–7. Answers will vary.